How to be a Christian
in Trying Circumstances

JMXturner.
1985.

How to be
a Christian
in Trying
Circumstances

Hugh Buckingham

EPWORTH PRESS

7162 0414 2

First published 1985
by Epworth Press
Room 195, 1 Central Buildings
Westminster, London SW1

Typeset by Gloucester Typesetting Services
and printed in Great Britain by
Richard Clay (The Chaucer Press) Ltd
Bungay, Suffolk

For Alison, Harriet and William

Contents

1 | The Believer, Goodness and God

A middle-aged couple, devoted members of their city church, decide one day that they would like to try and run a regular religious book-stall on the local Saturday covered market. 'It will be a means of spreading the Word of God,' they explain to their interested friends, 'and I expect we shall make a little money for the church too.'

They start with great enthusiasm and find, somewhat to their surprise, that it goes very well. They sell quite a few books, raise some money and most important of all make some helpful contacts with people unconnected with the church.

After a few weeks they find the regular commitment rather much and look round for help. A close friend agrees to assist and two members of the church's women's group offer some time once a month. It is still something of a burden, however, and the couple begin to grumble that the church is not giving them the support they deserve. They need a rota. So they go to their minister and ask him to announce in church one Sunday that they require volunteers. He does so and the couple also put a large notice on the church notice board saying, 'Please help!'

In some circumstances this may produce a whole lot of volunteers who work sweetly together for years. In many others, as here, nothing much happens. The minister, very sensibly, refuses to con-fuse matters by himself taking an active part in seeking volunteers and the responsibility remains with the couple whose decision it was to begin the project. They are beginning to feel dissatisfied and hurt.

The body of the church also looks on in some irritation. 'They decided to start the bookstall,' they say to one another, 'so it is up to them to get on with it.' They have a suspicion, which they cannot quite put into words, that there are other motives at work than simply to preach the gospel and to make some money for the church. The couple are not completely disinterested parties. They gain satisfaction from the success of their operation and seek some recognition of their merit in having started it. Though the couple have no intention of setting themselves up as superior and would swear blind that they are no better than anybody else in the church, yet there is an unconscious movement towards the delights of feeling pleased with themselves and the contrary discontent that few recognize their worth.

In due course the couple have succeeded in creating within the church a sense of guilt, or repressed anger, which is often much the same thing. They let their feelings be known with an 'At least I . . .' while the church responds with 'I'm sorry but . . .' ('You make me cross', 'I didn't choose your bookstall', 'Can't you see I'm busy', 'Why do you make me feel guilty?'). Or else there is a silent unease which quickly undermines the fellowship.

If the couple were not honestly seeking help but only a sense of their own rightness then any major response will discountenance them and they will get their own back by failing to organize a proper rota or by not giving the volunteers a reasonable job of work. This has the result of a rapid falling away of the helpers and, lo and behold!, the desired isolation of the originators who can now resume their grumbling with the added joy of now being able to say that the volunteers were of no help.

What has happened in this church is that some simple rules of human interaction have been flouted. Although the couple set up the bookstall for the sake of the church they were not deputized to do it. It is therefore entirely their initiative and they are responsible for its progress and outcome. It is neither for the church as a whole nor for the minister to act on their behalf in such a way as to create confusion about where accountability lies. Since neither the minister nor the church has chosen to set up a bookstall they have no duty to respond to its needs and need feel no sense of guilt if they do not. They may of course choose to assume responsibility for the project or to respond to a request for help, and there is no doubt that duties follow quickly upon such choices. But the nature and extent of the commitment should be clearly spelt out to, and if necessary negotiated with, those who offer their help, and requests must be, and must be seen to be, genuinely open-ended so that a 'yes' or a 'no' may be accepted with identical equanimity.

It is these sort of confusions, distortions and self-deceptions with which this book is concerned. Many outside the church will say at once, 'That is what we always thought. Church members are a bunch of hypocrites,' but that is to underestimate both the scale of hypocrisy outside the church and the peculiar difficulties under which the religious person labours. The former we must leave others to examine. Here we need to see why, since religious people are in most ways much the same as everybody else, they should tangle themselves in situations where they can be so quickly and easily accused of hypocrisy.

We can begin to answer that by isolating two very obvious factors in the lives of religious people which are peculiarly theirs. They are involved with morality, with good and evil, more intensely than their secular contemporaries, and they are involved with God. These two ingredients of the religious call need some initial examination.

A young man joins a Christian group by his own decision when he is in his early teens and is a happy member of it for a year or more. One day he arrives at the meeting-place to find that two of his fellow-members are involved in a brawl. Tempers have risen over some small matter, one side has hit out and the other has defended himself. The young man, outraged, goes to see his minister. 'Isn't this supposed to be a Christian community?' he explodes. Then how can such behaviour be countenanced? He has always believed that Christians are to love one another and here are two of them attacking each other. He cannot see his way to being a member of the group any longer. In vain does the minister point out that Christians are different from other people only in knowing, in principle, how to cope with disharmony not in living without it. The young man remains convinced that if, as he sees it, goodness has been breached by evil then Christianity is destroyed.

This is one of the major tensions that Christians have to live with. Good and evil exist alongside one another in all of us, but Christians are taught, often from their mother's knee (sometimes especially at their mother's knee) that they must be good. They know that when the little girl was bad 'she was horrid'. So they have to devise ways of coping with the badness to a degree not experienced by others who do not share their genuinely earnest desire to be good. There are many ways of dealing with badness within and all of them are treacherous. We can pretend that it is not there, gazing relentlessly into the heavenly kingdom. We can project it onto another individual or group so that they become the fall-guy for our own mischief. We can belabour ourselves until the guilt weighs with a frown upon every action we take. Even if we fly to forgiveness, the manoeuvres we execute are all too likely to end up where many of these battles finish – in self-righteousness. Living with good and evil is the first of the tortuous burdens that religious people shoulder when they take up their vocation.

And then there is that obstinate joker in the pack, God. God is by definition the Source and the Sustainer of all that is. He is behind all things, ahead of all things, under all things. It is impossible to think of a preposition which would not most felicitously describe God's relation to us. He cannot be argued with, knows no equal, stops all debate. We can choose to use his name in any way we wish and nobody can make a rational comeback. If it is this resource that we need at the moment then we can use him as excuse, pardoner, cornucopia, scourge, authority, puritan, spoilsport, to name just the few that come immediately to mind. The list can be expanded infinitely because God is – precisely – infinite.

It is not that the Christian is necessarily to be reproved for using God in these ways or in any other, though doubtless some are more helpful than others. Presumably any Christian will wish to attach to God that which he or she finds highest or most real in the religious vocation. Rather it is that Christians are often unaware how stifling God can be for others who do not share their faith, and at the same time stifling for themselves as well.

If Christians are seriously engaged in discussion or argument with an enquirer moments will arise when they are tempted to say, 'Well, I'm afraid that's something you just have to accept.' What these moments are will depend upon the sort of Christian faith they profess. Roman Catholics are likely to reach such moments a good deal more frequently than, say, a middle-of-the-road Church of England churchwarden, but each of them will invest their own propositions, few or many, with an absolute significance immediately behind which lies a God who cannot be refuted. It is like playing the joker in a card game. God's name brings down the shutters and enquirers are left feeling frustrated because they have either to 'just accept' what they are told or be seen to be arguing not just with a Christian but with God. Even if convinced they are right they will be left feeling they are, so to speak, wrong to be right because God cannot, by definition, be wrong. I believe that Christians seriously underestimate the furious impotence that much of their proselytism induces. If they have been brought up a Christian they have never known what it is like to be without God, even if they have rejected him later, and if they have been converted they often appear to have forgotten what their godless days were like.

Similarly God can, paradoxically, stifle the Christian's own growth. Not that God himself can in practice stifle anybody of course, but the way we use the God whom we have created in the image of our present condition prevents us from moving any further. It is not simply a question of accepting this doctrine or that. We do after all tend to adopt the faith which suits our social and psychological development. What happens is that we use the 'God says' as an excuse for not reaching out towards new ideas and possibilities as the clues accumulate. We use God to reinforce our prejudices rather than to spread our wings. So Christian morality turns into rules, Christian teaching into creeds and Christian worship into habit, and at every stage God is invoked to buttress our inertia.

The Christian's special difficulties then arise immediately out of his or her own profession of faith. The two main sources of the distortion of free Christian living are the way the Christian has to cope with the demand for goodness and the call to serve an omnipotent God. Much of the behaviour discussed later will time and again be seen to revolve around these ultimately insoluble problems of goodness and God.

Looking back, for instance, at the couple who started the market bookstall, we observe that the transaction was not a simple one. Most market stallholders straightforwardly seek a profit. They may enjoy their job or they may not, but the enjoyment of it is not often seen as anything more than a bonus. They are making a living. The couple, however, are not nearly so clear-headed. They need to make a surplus on their sales in order to keep their stall viable but they are not keeping the money. The money is being donated to a 'good' cause, the church, and they thereby entirely distance themselves from profit-making. Goodness has already taken the place of self-interest, money has become sanctified.

Furthermore they have stated that they have at least two other motives – to spread the Word of God through the Christian books that they are selling and to make personal contact with people who may express interest in the books though they are not practising Christians. The first is a purely godly sort of thing to do since it is ultimately God who will rejoice at people becoming godly, and the second is a good sort of thing to do since it appears obviously better that people should be, rather than should not be, members of the chu+ch.

The circumstances are now ripe for the distortion to take place. Giving away money they have earned, placing the Christian message before people and encouraging them to church membership puts the couple on one side of a divide and everybody else on the other. If they do not perceive the acute dangers of such a position and take account of it as they work out their Christian discipleship selling books, then all those who do not share their particular aspirations, even within their own 'good' community the church, will be made to appear ill-humoured, unhelpful, 'bad'. In some such way do the problems of God and of goodness present themselves in the daily life of the church.

Yet, even after it is acknowledged that God and goodness present a formidable hurdle, there may remain a sense of hurt that Christians, who after all believe they are moving towards truth, should be susceptible to so many self-deceptions. So at this stage it may be helpful to record some general notes of caution, even of comfort, which will be addressed to author and reader alike.

In the first place we must all take care that a bid to come to terms with our own self-deceptions does not add one more ideal to the many that the longsuffering Christian already carries. Most people have ideals of some sort; human beings seem to move inevitably in that direction. Yet the history of the world demonstrates how destructive ideals become, for people so quickly create gods out of them and build them into general principles which fix people into a straitjacket of their own making.

Conformity is purchased at the expense of freedom. The thrust of the endeavour becomes not the expansion of the ideal but the elimination of opposition. To safeguard ourselves against the tyranny of ideals we need to keep them under scrutiny, constantly asking ourselves the question, To whom do these ideals belong? And we would be wise to keep those ideals we feel we must retain short-term and specific rather than grandly universal. To imagine that we shall ever come to terms with all our self-deceptions is itself a delusion which can easily turn into a persecution of those who are not thought to attain the ideal. A couplet out of Gavin Ewart's gentle prayer/poem could perhaps stand as a petition for all idealists:

Lord I am not completely bad-mannered
Lord I am not a crusader mad-bannered.

Secondly, we must constantly recall that when we are dealing with people's motives, not just their behaviour patterns but with what those patterns conceal, then we are touching on some of the most sensitive areas of the human spirit. When we suggest that our motives are probably not what we think they are and that what those motives are we have not yet fully perceived, we may receive a response that operates at two levels.

It may strike a note in our conscious selves, either negatively or positively. We recognize the truth in what we have seen and consciously resolve to make some small shift in our behaviour, or contrariwise we shrug our shoulders, realizing that it is a truism long since learned or a perception that does not ring true for us.

We may, however, respond in some more subtle, less coherent way. We respond emotionally for reasons we do not quite understand. None of us is completely aware of the source of our emotions.

We cannot always be sure just why we are reacting in this or that emotional way. It takes us a lifetime to plumb the depths and even then we are only half-finished. We are half aware that our anger is always with particular people or actions or habits, or that we are envious, for reasons we have not quite thought through, of John but not of Michael. We are always being astonished at the fathomlessness of our behaviour, and receiving new light from unexpected sources.

I recall, for example a young woman – let us call her Ann – whom I saw on four occasions. She had been married for three years and, though there was no sexual infidelity on either side, things had been going from bad to worse. She scarcely spoke to her husband now, they had not been out together for months, did not want to make love and she was depressed and miserable. They had no children and the issue over whether to have any or not was a minefield that lay between them. Ann did not want children, she had no idea why. Her husband did and, in face of her obstinate refusal, had gone out a few months before and had bought himself a parrot to which he now gave devoted attention. I had little idea of how to help her, and Ann said that her husband had no intention of coming to see me. He did not want anybody interfering in his marriage, thank you, though she could do what she liked.

Those first two sessions Ann told me something about herself and her background and she seemed to find some relief in talking, though I made little contribution myself. When she came the third time I asked her about her father and she prevaricated, so I pressed. In a moment she was in floods of tears and she told me this story. She had loved her father and they had got on very well together though her memories of him were dim. One day when she was six years old she had been sitting with him in the lounge on opposite sides of the fire when he had suddenly cried out and died there and then. The family had rushed in and she was hurried out of the room and the same day sent away to stay with an aunt. She asked where her father was and her aunt told her that he had 'gone away on a journey', a message that was repeated when she returned home. After that, silence. Nobody, she said, had ever mentioned her father to her again, not even her mother. It was as if he had vanished into thin air. Her fright at the implicit prohibition about referring to him meant that she had never talked about him either and had 'put him out of her mind'.

She was as amazed as I was as she told me this story, almost the whole time in tears, because she had never mentioned her father to anybody since the day she came home after the funeral and she had had no conscious idea that he, and the way he had died, had affected her so much. She had not even thought much about him since that time.

She left then with a promise to return next week. When she came her whole face had changed. There was a bright smile and an inner alertness that had not been there before. She told me that her husband had taken her down to the pub during the week and things were ever so much better between them. She left me happy and I never saw her again.

What seemed to have happened was that somehow the complete blackout that had been imposed upon her memories of her father and the manner of his death had in its turn laid a blackout upon her. Her emotions and her capability of responding to emotions had been blocked by the well-meaning but damaging silence about her father. She did not want children because some sort of vague inner voice was telling her that she would not be able to cope with them. Children were the sort of beings to whom unmentionable disasters happened. She was caught in a trap into which she had drawn her husband, and it was only when the trap was sprung, as she allowed herself to speak about her father again and mourn for him, that her husband at last, with no understanding of what had happened, could yet begin to feel her coming free and so was able to take her out for the first time in months.

Most of our personal stories tend to be drabber than that, but it illustrates the sort of experience I am trying to get hold of. This second note of caution is that we shall be touching upon the edge of emotions some of which will be concealed in the depths of our unconscious. For ourselves this means that we must take that unknown part of ourselves into account. We must use, if we can, whatever tools are offered us to scatter a little of the darkness and bring a further harmony into our lives without imagining that the road to self-knowledge is anything less than arduous. We need to treat ourselves gently but with some dispassionate shrewdness.

More, though, it shows how careful we must be with other people. We cannot know what traumas others have hidden beneath apparently tranquil surfaces, and some of those traumas will fall over into the neurotic. The church, as a body that represents compassion and has a good father for its God, inevitably draws to itself, without a conscious motivation on their part, a more-than-average proportion of those who near some kind of neurosis. This is not the place to make any analysis of what those neuroses might be, even if it were within my competence to do so, which it is not, but the church needs to be vigilant in distinguishing the neurotic from normal disaffections. Neuroses need not just a warm heart and a clear head but more often professional advice as well.

Lastly we should take good care to remember that our strongest resistances appear wherever our convictions are most compelling. This may be because, after much labour, we have worked through and fined down our beliefs until we know what realities we can trust in, or it may be that here above all we are most, and dangerously defended. To distinguish the two is by no means always easy.

We are now in a position to examine more closely four areas in the life of the local church where Christians may catch themselves out in self-deceit. We look first at the way an individual may relate to the church as a whole, then at the strange ways in which money affects church members, and the next two chapters look at the relationship between minister and people and between one Christian and another. An additional chapter explains how deception is practised upon Christians by those who claim little or no faith, and the account ends by relating this approach to the insights of Jesus.

2 | The Believer and the Church

All believers who do not agree that 'You are nearer to God's heart in a garden than anywhere else on earth' have in due course to come to terms with the church. They have to decide such questions as what they want of a church and what sort of church it is that they want to join, what sort of people they will be expected to be or to become within their membership of that church, what they expect the prayer-life of the church to provide, and how to come to terms with the melancholy fact that the majority of their fellow-citizens think they are on a hiding to nothing. In this chapter we look at some of the ways in which Christians may deal with decisions of this nature.

How we choose a church

In the Western world there is a veritable Noah's Ark of local groups with which we may worship. Even the mainstream churches differ as widely within their own traditions as they do from one another. 'Closed' or 'open' membership, 'high', 'liberal', 'evangelical', 'charismatic', 'catholic', 'Bible-based' – the nuances are legion, hotly defended and to be found anywhere irrespective of the titular authority.

I recall visiting two Roman Catholic churches in France on the same day. The first was dimly-lit, full of candles and incense, women telling their beads in the back pew, a tiny three-foot 'nave' altar at the sanctuary steps dominated by the original ornate marble high altar. The second, filled with sun, was swept clean of every particle of furniture save a highly-painted altar free-standing in the centre of the church, and a priest strode round in jeans and a sweatshirt.

In addition to this diversity there is a major division between those churches which are in some sense national churches aiming to make themselves responsible for, or at least to show a presence in, every part of the country they represent, and congregational churches which aspire to do no more than offer a fellowship to those who follow their creed and practice. The Roman Catholic Church in Italy, the National Church in Sweden and the Anglican Church in England are examples of the former and it is the members of these sort of churches who are most prey to the difficulties that occur in choosing a church to worship in, though members of other churches could profit from pondering what follows. Indeed, the wider implications would lead us into a consideration of ecumenical issues which would be reckless in such pages as these.

Let us follow then Mr and Mrs Jones, a couple of practising Christians who live on the outskirts of one of the smaller cities. Mr Jones has been brought up in an Anglican church of a moderately high tradition. He is used to holy communion as the centre of worship, incense on feast days, not too many servers and auricular confession as a voluntary rather than a mandatory discipline. Mrs Jones was a nominal Methodist but was confirmed into the Anglican Church soon after marriage and has now become more enthusiastically high church than her husband. Their parish church, the Anglican church of the area in which they live, is of a central tradition. Communion is the main act of worship on a Sunday but there is a family service on occasions with young people playing guitars, no encouragement to make one's confession, a dull magazine and it is, as they say to one another after trying it out for a couple of Sundays, 'rather cliquey'.

They make a few enquiries and hear of a couple of churches in the city where they might worship in the sort of way to which they have become accustomed. They try them both out and settle in the end for St Augustine's. The people are pleased to see them, the church is nice and warm and, though a little higher than Mr Jones likes, it suits Mrs Jones very well and Fr Robinson preaches excellent sermons. So they become St Augustine's people and will probably end up closely involved in church councils, fetes and missions.

That is a common sort of instance but it can easily be Tom who 'doesn't like these new-fangled services', Dick who 'considers the minister far too right-wing for me' and Harry who 'can't abide all those children running about the church' or Polly who 'has always liked a small village church', Dolly who 'does find it difficult to pray with all those statues about the place' or Molly who 'likes to hear the real Gospel being preached'. The accidents of birth, temperament, upbringing and geography all have their part to play, quite apart from elements of long-standing or recent conviction, and it is not to be denied that there may be exceptional circumstances which make it fitting that these considerations should override all others. There are, however, the strongest temptations to disregard, or not to be aware of, some important underlying factors.

One of the central insights of the Christian faith is that growth and pain are intimately related. Not that all pain, or all kinds of pain, can or will lead to growth; rather it is that growth is, more often than not, accompanied by an attending hurt. The world does not teach us that. In the world it is strength and achievement that matter. We learn to crawl, walk, talk. We go to school to be taught to read, write and number, to pass examinations, attain perhaps the heights of a university. We must marry well, make a good home, climb the ladder of success. We always succeed if we win.

It is not so easy to grasp that at the back of every step forward there lies a pain. Some of these pains, particularly at the beginning of life, cannot be avoided. The scream of indignation which brings the newborn child out of the comfortable ambience of the womb into the hard, air-breathing world is echoed in later years in the tears of frustration when the sums will not come right, the hurt when our gifts do not match up to our ambitions, the labour to come to terms with death. Nobody can avoid being born, going to school, growing up and coping with loss, and the presence of these imperatives ensures that even the facile and the glib must occasionally confront the grim realities.

Most of us try a bit harder than that. We discipline ourselves to attain the educational standards that we require. We refuse, at some cost, a succession of easy sexual encounters in order to discover ourselves and our neighbours within the framework of a committed life. We go out of our way to help lame dogs over stiles when it would be more comfortable to pass by on the other side. But although there is an element of pain in all those experiences, they are all basically self-enhancing and we labour at them because we can see some advantage in them for ourselves or because they make us feel good. The real pain, and therefore in the Christian understanding the real growth, comes when, having reached a point of impotence, we stop pretending, lower our defences and permit ourselves to be revealed as we are. Against the bitter opposition of our own will, we admit our needs, share our failures and open ourselves to welcome the love that others will give us.

When we choose an environment which gives the least possible resistance to our natural humanity we are refusing to take that path and therefore we are refusing to grow. We do not want our dearest convictions or habits or principles to be at the risk of change. We do not wish to meet people who entertain unfamiliar ideas and indulge in novel practices, who might invite us to a way of loving that we do not relish. We need to be safe and not to give admission to any growth which does not arise from inside that security. We do not want to face the possibility of being shaken, hurt or disarmed. So we choose to stay with that which is familiar and everybody loses. We deprive ourselves of the opportunity of making new discoveries, and we do not allow the local church the chance to examine itself afresh in the light of the people we are and the ideas we represent. We have failed to understand that Christian community is formed in the battle to love our enemies.

And if it is a flight from ourselves it can also be an attempt to escape into a personalized religion which is not rooted in the community. If people come to worship in a neighbourhood church where they themselves live they bring with them the joys and anxieties of that locality, its problems, its factories, its homes. Then the church becomes, or at least strives to become, harnessed to a way of life which is understood and lived by its own members. When people worship wherever they feel inclined they may create a church disengaged from its foundations. There is a tacit consensus that the church is a private hobby for the religiously inclined.

Choosing is a gift we have been granted by our Creator and the gospels are unyielding in their belief that our exercise of that gift is of the most crucial importance. To choose churches like restaurants is not to avail ourselves of the gift but to repudiate its seriousness.

The obvious way for ministers to neutralize such behaviour is for them to discourage people from becoming members of a church other than the local worshipping unit of their denomination unless there are reasons which are both compelling and fully discussed between the participants. Naturally ministers are most reluctant to do this. Enthusiastic Christians are hard enough to come by these days without looking a gift horse in the mouth, and some ministers, far from discouraging such worshippers, go out of their way to advertise their wares as attractively and widely as possible. The price may be the acceptance of an unhealthy dilettantism in Christian faith and practice.

Boxed into the church

A feature of an industrialized society is the way people's lives become compartmentalized. Farmers and housewives still live where they work, maintaining a unity between all parts of their lives, but most others inhabit at least two worlds, domestic and occupational, and they have less control over the latter. At home they are an indispensable member of a small group, exercising a crucial function in the family; at work they are an insignificant part of a machine, which can be replaced without disturbing the structure. Different conventions apply in each place and people become used to switching from one to the other. A businessman at home may be punctilious over paying his bills without delay, while at work he will make it a policy to maintain liquidity by settling accounts at the last possible moment. A working mother may slap her junior-age child for uttering swear words she thinks nothing of using herself in the factory. With a minimal sense of incongruity they will live in two different worlds, like the manager who, though he worked only five minutes from where he lived, always went the long way back at the end of the day to give himself time to adjust to the home and its norms.

Religion, which was once as natural a part of the whole of life as breathing, has become another segment of a person's life. Though every Christian is aware that a Christianity divorced from life is barren, the very words we use about it demonstrate their separation. We say that we must 'try to relate Christian faith to everyday life'. Ministers writing a sermon labour to find 'an example from everyday life' or beg their audience to 'go out into the world' as if the world were a menacing jungle from which, in church, we are momentarily protected. Religion, even for the zealous, seems to bear upon the rest of existence in the same sort of way as money earned at work enables the family to be maintained at home. The commodity is bundled from one sphere to the other. The relation between them is practical, not intrinsic. So worship, instead of being the narrow part of an hour-glass through which passes the sand of all our life, becomes an end in itself, an act that defines us as religious rather than defining our religion.

All the world accepts that the spheres of work and the home have an equal validity and are a necessary counterbalance for one another, which is why there is always such widespread anxiety over the level of unemployment. Religion is an optional extra which can only be verified from within. Many people rarely give religion more than a passing thought and do not accept that it has much, if any, relevance to the way we live our lives, and there is, to be truthful, a great deal that tells against a religious interpretation of life. And so there come times in the lives of Christians when the effort to bring religion and life together becomes more than we can manage. We sink back upon God crying, 'Underneath are the everlasting arms.' A recognition and acceptance of our dependence upon God is indeed an ineluctable component of our Christian faith but when we use it to avoid facing honestly the incongruities between what we believe, or are bidden to believe, and how we live, we are deceiving ourselves.

The temptation to do so is great because the challenges to

Christian faith today are formidable. Those challenges are intellectual, moral and confessional.

Many of our intellectual difficulties give the appearance of having arisen at about the time of Darwin, and that perception is true to the extent that it was the careful scholarship of Darwin which most conspicuously forced the church to examine its presuppositions in the light of the emerging scientific view of the world. Partly though, his work also coincided with the beginning of universal education so that today every member of the church has to come to terms with arguments and scholarship which in previous eras they were content to leave to the clergy. Modern biblical criticism, for instance, is both complex and disputatious. It requires some intellectual effort to begin to look at the Bible in this new, scientific way. I suppose that the majority of Christians are still in the position I was in when I first went up to university to read theology having been a practising member of the church all my life. I went my first term to a series of lectures on form criticism (a particular way of analyzing the Gospels) which might as well have been given in Greek for all the sense they made to me. I had no idea at all what the lecturers were talking about. It was my first introduction to a completely new way of looking at not just the Bible but the whole of the Christian faith. Everybody may find the time and the will to adjust to this new way of looking at the Christian faith according to their capacity, but the temptation is to leave religion in its box, to learn to live with the nagging worry that science may be proving religion untrue, and to hope that it may last out our lifetime.

Morally the issues are so much wider than they used to be. It used to be enough to live by the ten commandments and the dominical requirement that we should love God and our neighbour. The moral problems that arose in our lives and within our families we resolved by those simple, comprehensible rules. Today we are expected to have thought about, and to take up a position about, such contentious questions as homosexuality, abortion, feminism, church schools and the work ethic. National debates like these broaden into international affairs and we are faced with human rights, nuclear disarmament and all the headaches about the

North/South debate. Such issues do not submit to a simple rule of thumb and we become tangled in their complexity.

Faith itself is strongly under fire. So many people do not believe any more and take us for simple-minded or worse if we do. The scientific bent of the world which has a hold upon all our minds encourages us to try and find proofs of our faith. We want our faith, need it, to be respectable and explicable. At the same time we are aware that walking by faith inhabits a different sort of world. Science cannot evaluate faith as it can a cabbage. The two worlds overlap within us and as we pause irresolute on the fence between them, the idle and fearful part of us bids us play safe, dodge the tension and fall back upon:

Immortal, invisible, God only wise,
In light inaccessible, hid from our eyes.

We deceive ourselves in fact, and it becomes most commonly apparent in the church service. It is a necessary part of an act of worship, as I said earlier in this section, that it should define the religion it practises. Worship therefore has to be to some degree declaratory. It needs to proclaim, and to invite the worshippers to participate in proclaiming, the foundations of its faith. So creeds, readings from the sacred works and communal acts of praise are unavoidable ingredients of an act of worship. But when they are the only ingredient, when it is implied right from the beginning of the service that the church is assembled not just to 'come apart and rest awhile', which is an invaluable part of worship, but to enter into a different sphere of existence, alarm bells should begin to ring in our ears.

The preacher quotes from the Bible, applying each of its statements precisely to the problems and anxieties and faith of today. He or she makes no more than a slight attempt to place the quotations in context and does not explain what the words might have meant to its listeners two thousand years ago. It is as if the last hundred years of biblical scholarship never existed. Every word of Jesus is quoted as if it was fed into a tape recorder from his lips, St John's Gospel, almost universally agreed to contain strong elements of meditative reflection, being used in precisely the same way as the others. There is no evaluation of the different books of the Bible or discrimination between the quotations in those books except that those passages which appear to be spiritual, in or out of context and however inaccurate the translation, are used to uplift the congregation and the offensive parts, especially those concerning violence or sex or which portray God as rather less than pleasant, are tacitly ignored. Justification for such behaviour is sought in some such phrase as, 'We mustn't disturb the faith of the little ones' without considering whether it might not be more rewarding to help the little ones to grow up.

The minister is often encouraged by the congregation to play the game. To strive to bring some accord between the worlds of science and religion, or to look beyond homespun moralistic judgments, or to grapple with the reality of God and how he might be present in the world, is more than we bargain for. We have no wish for our faith to be taken with a deep seriousness, only with an appropriate solemnity. So we pass out of church with a smile and a 'Good sermon, pastor,' with some relief leaving the unattainable ideals back in church till next week. Sometimes even, as we shall see in a later chapter, there is a fear that any disturbance of such assumptions might undermine the minister's own faith.

Outside formal worship there are numerous opportunities for us to continue such behaviour wherever we encounter religion in a secular setting. A religious publisher, for example, produced a year or so ago a slim, beautifully presented volume setting out some of the great themes of the Bible for the junior-school child. It began naturally with creation, and the double-page spread, well-drawn and colourful, showed a handsome Adam and Eve in a country setting surrounded by giraffes, hippopotami and other modern animals. The volume was not from a fundamentalist publisher, who might have honestly believed that creation began in 4004 BC, but was intended for general distribution, and the salesman who was recommending it to ministers in their homes said that so far it had received universal approbation. He was startled and not at all prepared to listen when it was pointed out to him that any moderately well-informed eight-year-old could have told him that animals did not exist in that form when man first appeared on earth and

that it might have been helpful to offer some historical verisimili-
tude to questing minds. He and the ministers he visited preferred
to stand fast by the myth because it was too hazardous a venture to
begin looking at the reality of the world that lies behind the myth.
The worlds of religion and life were better kept separate.

It requires both vigilance and courage to resist the temptations
of this approach to the religious experience, as much within ourselves as among our fellow-Christians.

Evasive prayer in the church

What effect we expect our prayers to have depends upon what we
believe prayers are capable of doing. Broadly there are two distinct
stances: what we might call the supernaturalist/interventionist one,
and the immanentist/human freedom one. The first sees God at all
times acting directly upon the world. He is personal, concerned,
aware, and always ready to respond positively to the prayers of the
faithful. He is the Father who cares for all his people and may be
approached at any time for help, though like a human father, he
has a certain arbitrariness of spirit, or in any case so it appears to
us. For we cannot be sure what the answers to our prayers will be
since the Father has knowledge of factors which are not apparent
to us. He has to take into account the immaturity of our development, which means that we shall be asking for the wrong things in
the wrong way at the wrong time, and also all the other prayers
which are addressed to him, or not addressed to him but which he
is aware of, which in turn will affect how he responds to us. God is
a person, this view believes, who intervenes in this world's affairs,
is willing and able to answer our prayers intelligibly, and one way
or another without question will always do so.

The immanentist/human freedom view does not understand God
to be related to the world in quite that 'He over there – we over
here' way. God is part of the fabric of the world and his working is
to be seen through the realities, and in particular through the
human beings of that world. He is the energy that keeps bringing
new life to us – into our fields through the cycle of the seasons, into
our arms as we nurture our children and into our hearts as we keep

learning new facets of the religious quest. He is still a personal Father, not to be confused with his creation, but the means of his working is the creation he has brought into being. We are his hands, his feet, his eyes. It is not possible, this view urges, to see God in any other light if we are to preserve human freedom. We cannot be both free and subject to arbitrary manipulation from without.

There are Christians who are implacably supernaturalist. If they lose their pencil they will pray to God and they will at once find it. If they need £1400 for some cause which they are convinced is an authentic charge upon them from God they will expect God to make it immediately available. They live by faith, they say, and there are enough recorded instances of the success of such a way of life to keep us from scoffing. Those convinced of its legitimacy, however, should note there is the strongest temptation to indulge in all sorts of equivocations when matters do not quite turn out as we expect. If the £1400 we need does not arrive, then in order to maintain our framework we shall have to find arguments which will enable us to contain the non-appearance of the money within our overall scheme. These arguments will probably have to do with our lack of faithfulness in prayer or life, our blindness in asking for the wrong thing, or God having some greater plan which he will reveal in due course. Any logical evaluation of the position or of its defences is in any case quite impossible. All it needs for its mainten- ance is enough to happen as a result of prayer for it to be validated in our own estimation. Its foundation is that the human being does nothing except ask and God does everything else.

Other Christians are equally resolutely immanentist, though most holding that position would not follow the rigorous logic of Don Cupitt in his book *Taking Leave of God*.

Prayer is a way of opening ourselves to the requirement that we have laid upon ourselves and meditating upon the ideals and values to which we have committed ourselves. We seek strength to meet adversity, love to give to our neighbour, courage and determination to overcome sloth and depression, and the will to will our own inner change. In quiet recollection we seek simplicity and clarity of mind so that the forces of renewal can do their healing work in us. In several senses of the phrase, *we pray for ourselves* and we have to answer our own prayers, for it is <u>superstition</u> to suppose that our prayers will be answered apart from our own efforts.*

This is not a religionless but a godless Christianity which does not reflect the reliable experience of many who are immanentist by temperament or conviction. The foundation of this view is that God can do nothing and the human being must do everything.

Most of us, I suppose, are somewhere in the middle between the supernaturalist and the immanentist view. We feel warmly towards the remark made, I believe, by William Temple when he said that all he knew was that when he prayed things started to happen and when he did not they stopped. However, that remark is capable of an austere supernaturalist or immanentist interpretation. His prayers, when they occurred, might have meant that God could now intervene because he had asked him to do so or that he was rooting himself once again in God and so became free to hear and follow the religious call.

And here at last, after this long but necessary introduction, we are in a position to see how Christian prayer can be used as an evasion rather than a means of grace. It is not so used by those who hold either a strict supernaturalist or a strict immanentist view of God since they have no need of it. It is rather the position of those who are not sure where they stand, or who have not sufficiently thought it through. They use their uncertainties in order to avoid their responsibilities.

A simple example is the person who goes to church and prays with earnest concentration for the poor and hungry and declines next day to make any contribution towards the poor of the Third World because internally he or she has convinced him or her self that the prayer is sufficient demonstration of concern. Or of the church which makes similar prayers and refuses to hold in view the political implications of living in a world where there are ample resources for the earth's population were they shared between us all.

* Don Cupitt *Taking Leave of God,* SCM Press 1980, p. 131.

'The church should not interfere in politics' is only an honest argument if at the same time the church does not pray about such matters either.

It is quite common, too, in home and office. An ambitious businessman with a young family spends a long day at the office and usually brings back work to do in the evenings. His family are not surprised, though they are worried, when he falls ill with what the doctors diagnose to be a stomach ulcer they suspect is caused through strain and overwork. His wife, a devout Christian, quite fittingly prays for him. However, if the diagnosis is correct, it means that something will have to be done about the husband's attitude to his work and the best person to tackle that difficulty is his wife. That presents problems because the wife knows that her husband's ambitions are tied up very closely with how he sees himself as a person and she does not know what a curtailment of his ambition might mean in human terms, especially as it affects herself and her family. She does not want to face that problem with all the disenchantment it may bring, so she prays yet more earnestly. This keeps the problem important, might even make it look as if something is being done, while allowing her to avoid it. The level of indignation if she is challenged on the point will indicate whether she is playing this game. Her cross rejoinder will be something like, 'Well, I've got to pray for him, haven't I?' (just as in the opposite position she might say, 'Well, God helps those who help themselves, doesn't he?'). She is shifting up and down the scale between pure supernaturalist and pure immanentist conviction in order to avoid the dilemma. Prayer becomes not a toil but an evasion.

A strange crowd of people pass through ministers' studies and such behaviour is at home there. Troubles, straightforward enough on the surface, frequently have deep roots and many a time a minister is quickly foxed. He would be advised to pass them on to somebody more competent, but ministers are often reluctant to do that. It is easier to say, 'Shall we pray about it?' or 'I should go away and pray about it'. It is not easy for the suppliant to defy such a suggestion for, though he might have wished for something more helpful, it can hardly be expected that ministers should not wish to encourage prayer. The same ploy is used by ministers when they are confronted with a person who makes them feel frightened. Perhaps the visitor is unwittingly treading on ground which the minister finds personally very sensitive, or by the strength of his or her personality makes the minister feel inadequate. These feelings are better examined, but many ministers fall to prayer instead, thereby neatly upstaging the visitor. It is not that prayer is always inappropriate, but that it can easily be used as a defence, and the justification for the defence is to push prayer further up the scale towards stark supernaturalism.

It is relatively simple to withstand somebody, usually a minister, who plays the game with us. 'Would you like to pray about it?' 'No, thank you very much, but what I would like . . .'. To the degree that we ourselves are caught up in the theological dilemma we need to sit down and consider carefully once again whereabouts on the spectrum our beliefs about prayer stand.

The Gaussian victory

Herman Wouk's novel *The City Boy* describes the childhood experiences of a young boy, Herbie, brought up in downtown New York. Mr Gauss is Herbie's headmaster and much of the action takes place in some barren countryside outside New York where Mr Gauss takes Herbie and many of his school-fellows for a two months' camp in the summer holidays. One of the regular features of the camp is a day's sports contest against another group of campers who invariably trounce Mr Gauss's boys. This day Mr Gauss's teams have been defeated 45–35 in basketball and 43–12 in baseball, though one of their team, Lennie, has done rather well. Mr Gauss is later that evening addressing his campers in the hall. Camp Manitou is the Gaussian team and Camp Penobscot their opponents.

'I want to tell you, boys and girls,' went on Mr. Gauss, 'that today Camp Manitou was *not defeated*.'

There was a stunned stillness for a moment, then a tumult of yells and clapping. Mr. Gauss permitted the noise for perhaps thirty seconds, then quieted it with a raised hand.

'I saw those games,' he declaimed. 'I know how the score read. And still I say to you campers of Manitou we did not lose today. *We won.*'

More cheers. Herbie, not quite knowing what Mr. Gauss meant, but sensing a vague wonderful meaning in his words, cheered too.

'Boys and girls, there are victories in the scoreboard sense, and there are victories in the moral sense. George Washington at Valley Forge won a victory in the moral sense. General Custer in his last stand won a victory in the moral sense. Moses, standing on the mountains of Moab, seeing the Land of Promise which he could not enter, won a victory in the moral sense. If Washington was truly defeated, if Custer was truly defeated, if Moses was truly defeated, then today Camp Manitou was defeated. But if those great heroes of history each won a great victory – *and you know that they did* – then today Camp Manitou won a great victory!'

Herman Wouk dubs this kind of victory a Gaussian victory and goes on to write:

Strangely enough, the speech of the owner of Camp Penobscot, welcoming his returning teams that night, was very much shorter, and the rival camp was full of buoyant hilarity for days after the contest, all unaware that they had undergone such a Gaussian trouncing. That is the unique charm of a Gaussian victory. It elates the 'winning' side, and does not in the least depress the other.

Later that evening Wouk has the boys see through Mr Gauss in this whispered conversation in the dormitory:

. . . At last Ted said hoarsely, 'Hey, guys, ain't ol' Gauss a real bag o' hot air?'

'You bet! An' how! What a stinker!' came a husky chorus in reply.

'All that boloney about a victory,' said Ted. 'We got skunked. Who was he kiddin'?'

'Them Penobscots murdered us,' said one boy in the darkness . . . The lads tossed and fidgeted until one by one they dropped

asleep. Poor boys! The trouble with a Gaussian victory is that
its aftertaste is so miserable. Honest defeat honestly swallowed is
a bitter dose, but a clean brief one . . .*

One has only to tell the story in our context for there to come
flooding into one's mind the sermons of dignitaries at the introduction of a new minister to a church, of ministers at annual general
meetings, of the lay chairman of the local men's group and of the
church's statisticians at headquarters. Most of us at times refuse to
face unpleasant facts, but the unique quality of a Gaussian victory
is that unpleasant facts are stood on their head and made into
pleasant ones. More than that, they are actually seen to be an
advance on their opposite so that it becomes more noteworthy to
have failed than to have succeeded.

So the district church official pays a visit to a local church where
the regular congregation has decreased from fifty to twenty-three
over five years and, because there is a newer and livelier church
within three miles, looks like going even lower. The district church
council has examined the situation and has decided that it is un-
economic to keep a small and dying church open any longer when
there is an alternative so close, and has requested their official to
convey their decision to the church. The message he is bringing is
therefore, 'You are too small and getting smaller. We can't afford
to keep you open any longer and you are going to have to close.'
However, saying that to families who have worshipped in the same
building for fifty years or more is not going to be very agreeable so
he sets out to bring about a Gaussian victory.

He brings with him a batch of statistics he has carefully prepared beforehand, and he begins by telling the gathered members
of the church that statistics prove that the numbers of people in
their church nationally has increased by eight per cent in the last
five years. They are members of a growing church, living in a
generation where there is an exciting movement of the Spirit.
Among those eight per cent, he continues, the average age of all
new members is forty-three years, and his hearers have an impres-

* Quotations from Herman Wouk, *The City Boy*, Cape 1956 (Fontana
1973), pp. 194, 197, 202–3. © Herman Wouk 1956.

sion of a hoard of vigorous men and women in their prime flocking into the church. He does not tell them, however, that that statistical average is made up of a majority of people aged fifty-five years and over together with a much smaller number of eighteen to nineteen year olds who bring the average age sharply down. In the district, he says, there has been a small decline of five per cent over the same period but they can take it from him that many of the people who have left have been 'dead wood' and the church is now slimmer and healthier as is proved by the fact that donations have risen fourteen per cent in that time.

Next, he turns to the other church three miles away to which the congregation are to be encouraged to become attached. He pictures to them a lively, happy church with the full-time minister, an excellent preacher, they have been unable to afford. The church is warm and in no need of the repairs theirs so conspicuously requires and there were, when he last heard, no less than thirteen church groups they can join as well as the opportunity they will now have to take part in the wider community activities that a large population allows. Moreover the disposal of this dilapidated church will not only lift an enormous burden from their shoulders but the church will also gain from the sale since the building could raise as much as £16,000.

His peroration goes something like this. 'My friends, brothers and sisters! What a privilege it is for us to be living in this era! With the instant modern communications this age has been so richly endowed with, we are taking the glorious message of the gospel to every corner of the globe. Our message is being heard – and, friends, being acted on – in world-wide terms more than in any other generation before us. The church is strong, vigorous and growing, and now you have an opportunity to take part in that growth. By joining yourselves to our friends down the road your faith will blossom and flower like the good seed in the good earth and God's name will be glorified from one end of the earth to the other.'

That is a Gaussian victory in its simple form, an attempt to use any device, from angels and archangels downwards, to turn defeat into victory, plain failure into apparent success. The heart of the

Christian message is what appears to be an uncomplicated trans-
formation of defeat into victory. Jesus, the picture is painted, goes
to the cross, his head held high, determination written on his brow,
unyieldingly resolved to suffer whatever lies ahead of him. He goes
to his death like a hero, the empty tomb already casting its light
over the shadow of the cross. We with a similar courage must face
whatever suffering or defeats that God brings us so that we too may
be uplifted, ennobled like our Master. Failure, in the image of the
Lord, is not failure at all for God is already bringing victory out
of defeat.

Sometimes that which is more near the truth is most misleading.
Unquestionably there is a deep paradox about defeat and victory
within the Christian faith but it is not a simplistic one. Blithely to
anticipate victory in defeat is like taking a cut flower, sticking it in
the ground and expecting it to grow. The flower has only appeared
through a long process of growth, tangling with its environment,
withstanding its competitors. God may turn victory into defeat,
may indeed find defeat to be a victorious sort of experience, but he
does it in his own way and his own time. We can count on God's
victory but not necessarily on ours.

To try to bring about a Gaussian victory, then, is an attempt to
put the cart before the horse, to avoid living through the experience
of failure, loss and collapse, to try and enjoy the blossom before we
have tilled the soil. Such an easy way out of hurt naturally finds
plenty of people to justify it and one of the most popular ways is to
claim that it is necessary to encourage people when they are in
trouble. The church official quoted would doubtless use this argument and feel it most genuinely. Yet as Herbie and his companions
demonstrate, though people are temporarily elated, they shortly
become a good deal more disgruntled than they were before. 'Hey,
guys,' says Ted within a few hours of Mr Gauss's famous speech,
'ain't ol' Gauss a real bag o' hot air?' People quickly see through a
Gaussian victory and 'its aftermath is so miserable'.

If the people in the dying church had wanted encouragement
they would probably have preferred that the official should first of
all have made an honest acknowledgement of the facts as they were
discussed in the district church council, without hiding or exagger-

ating either side of the question. They would have liked a sympathetic understanding of their position, an admission of how hurtful it is to bear the loss of a fellowship and a building they have known and loved over many decades. And finally they would have liked some assistance, or promise of assistance, with all the arrangements for the handover without any attempt to take the responsibility for these matters out of their hands. Even better, they may have liked the district church council to have initiated open-ended discussions with them before ever a decision to close the church was made.

Fortunately it is not at all difficult to counteract such behaviour in the church. If you can imagine yourself present at the district church official's meeting and, when he has finished, saying out loud the rudest word you will permit yourself to utter, the balloon collapses without trace! It is such openly pretentious behaviour that a ribald exclamation followed by an honest exchange of opinions and views will nearly always clear the air. Of course anger may get the better of us and ribaldry turn into abuse, but perhaps that is better than moody resentment carried around for generations and expressed in Ted's out-of-hearing remark, 'We got skunked. Who was he kiddin'?'

3 | The Believer and Money

The world has always enjoyed riches when it can get them, but this generation of the Western world is the first to have such universal access to the riches that the world offers and the first to interpret wealth almost exclusively in terms of money. 'What is it worth?' or 'What is he worth?' is the currency we use. I recall the complete bewilderment of a pair of businessmen who ran a medium-sized brewery when questioned about the purposes for which they conducted their business. They ran it to make a profit, they said. When every consideration had been taken into account about the vital necessity of making a profit they still could not see that there might be any purpose beyond that one. It was not that they were unconvinced about the social and community functions that their business might offer, they simply could not make head nor tail of what the questioner was talking about.

Jesus claimed that 'You cannot serve God and Mammon'. When he talked of 'mammon' he would have been thinking in the wider context of the inheritances to which all the young male Jews he was addressing would have been looking forward. In most modern versions of the Bible the word 'mammon' has been translated 'money' or even 'Money', and although this does not truly reflect the historical context, it does accurately reproduce the modern feeling of the Greek word which means 'that which is trusted in'. Jesus then was saying that trust in God and trust in wealth are incompatible.

So, although the church has therefore always been awkwardly placed in a wealth-producing society, it has never been more so than now. It is deeply affected by the culture it inhabits. It talks of the cost-effectiveness of an educational programme, of maximizing its investments and about discount purchasing schemes. It throws up financial servants of the church with names like the Ecclesiastical Insurance Office. It is caught on the horns of a dilemma. It needs money in really quite large quantities in order to keep itself in business and has to rely for its supply on the generosity of either the charitable donations of its members or, in a few cases, the generosity of deceased benefactors. Yet it has a mandate from its master which says that riches are extraordinarily dangerous and might best be renounced altogether. It has to live in the real world – to make realistic budgets, to pay its servants a reasonable salary, to finance excellent initiatives. It has also to live with the fact that it is easier for a camel to pass through the eye of a needle than for a rich man to enter the kingdom of God.

In this predicament Christians are found to be juggling with their motives or compartmentalizing their Christian practice. They try to balance prudence with generosity or renunciation with life insurance policies and end up living unrealistically in both worlds. This can be demonstrated by examining the antithetical attitudes towards money given in the second and third sections of this chapter and by reflecting how easily we shift from one to the other without breaking step.

Stewardship

Stewardship has been a paramount discovery of the last twenty-five years of the church's life. It began with a small number of professional fundraising organizations who had stumbled on the fact that the churches were desperate for money but inefficient and bashful about raising it. Their startling success soon had the church setting up its own organizations to avoid paying the professionals' hefty fees. At the same time, because of its faint unease where money was concerned, the church made some attempt to widen the content of stewardship to include, as the catch-phrase went, 'time and talents'. Church members were urged to give very much more substantially than they had in the past and at the same time to offer what personal gifts they had, what talents and skills, to their neighbours and their church. The venture has never looked back. The church now receives an annual income that previous generations would have thought a fantasy and many churches have neighbourhood schemes and lively church groups arising directly out of what are still known as stewardship campaigns.

The principles have been conceded long ago and there are few churches left which have not been affected by the stewardship movement. The cost has been high, though. Wherever the scheme has been introduced it has engaged the strong emotions of all those who have been asked to participate and antagonisms have been common. The reason why people have been so upset has usually been put down to their reluctance to part with their money, and there can be no doubt that many people, particularly among those who have only begun to enjoy the fruits of their labours in recent decades, have taken some time to start thinking realistically about giving in a society which can no longer rely upon the squire's patronage.

To stop at that rather censorious judgement, however, is less than just. There are at least two other reasons why Christians have been unhappy about stewardship. First, they have felt in an ill-defined sort of way that it is indecent to bring money out into the open in this way. They have felt this especially because there has been a more or less implied demand in most campaigns that, since people should give according to their means, they are therefore expected to reveal the strengths and weaknesses of their own financial position. This demand has always generated strong resistance and churches have fallen over backwards to accommodate people with all kinds of promises about leak-proof security.

There is another, even more inarticulate, impression. People have often sensed that they are the victims of a kind of unintentional confidence trick. Christians generally do not have any difficulty with the basic concept of stewardship which the church has suddenly discovered. Once it has been presented to them that they do not possess anything of their own but that they stand as guardians and caretakers of it all on behalf of God, they are perfectly prepared to understand and adopt such a principle. After all in some country areas there are still men called 'stewards' who on behalf of the owner have the oversight of a farm and its men. Stewardship is not difficult. But they have a hunch that this is not what the church is really talking about, for the church is not using its discovery to illuminate the Christian's relationship to the world, which is the logic of teaching about stewardship, but is rather on its own behalf making a bid for the Christian's money, time and talents – especially money. However visionary and religious its language, the church has been essentially seeking its own ends. Even where the focus of the effort has lain outside the church, as it often has with community initiatives and so on, the demand has been for the Christian to act from and on behalf of the church. The ends have been unimpeachable (because most people can easily be brought to a realistic understanding of church budgetting and of the needs of the community), but the means to those ends have become distorted.

Furthermore, the church has been presenting the teaching in such a way as to ensure that it gets the best of the arguments and is never seen to be in the wrong. It has been easy for the church to interpret either of the second two arguments in terms of the first. That is to say, if Christians have been able to articulate their doubts about the church giving an undue emphasis to money or about the way the church uses the word stewardship misleadingly, the church has always been able to say – or more likely ruefully suggest – that Christians are using these arguments because they are too mean to give the church any more than they do at present. Nobody can disprove that response except by giving the church more money, time and talents, by which action they appear to be totally conceding the church's original contention. So whatever happens and whatever the Christian does, the church comes off best and he is made to feel guilty.

It works out in practice like this. The fund-raiser, who may be local lay person, minister or a professional appointed by the wider church, supported by a small number of co-opted helpers, announces that the church requires an extra £X the following year to carry out its responsibilities in church and community. A corpus of literature is assembled and a canvass arranged among the members of the church. The literature will have a heavy emphasis upon God and his call. Texts like, 'God so loved the world that he gave his only-begotten Son' and 'His inestimable love in the redemption of the world by our Lord Jesus Christ' are used as the heart of the submission. If God gave so much, how can we give less?

An appeal like that cannot be questioned without appearing uncommitted, mean or at the very least disloyal, for it speaks to the very highest motives. But neither on the other hand can it be honestly and genuinely responded to except by doing what Jesus suggested to the rich young man, renouncing everything and following him, and since few will be prepared, or are in a position, to do that, the rest are inevitably left feeling in some way inadequate. The fund-raisers speak from a position of such high endeavour, such impregnability, that virtually any response less than the ultimate surrender is bizarre. How can £12 a month and one evening a week compare with Jesus' sacrifice on the cross?

Nonetheless there are satisfactions to be gained on the other side of the equation too. An appeal to example has often been a feature of the campaigns. Mr Smith and the Reverend Brown have pledged so much of their income per month. How exhilarating for them to be placed in such prominence! Others can share their satisfaction by approximating as closely as possible to their level of giving, after taking into account of course all the factors that make these exemplars uniquely capable of generosity. We have now pledged nearly as much as the most generous members of the church, they can whisper to themselves, so we can assume ourselves to be among the most sacrificial of the congregation.

A flood of pamphlets rains upon the church demonstrating that the basis of the appeal has not changed much in the last twenty-five years. To illustrate this I quote from one of them which is a recent standard production from an English diocese. It argues in an opening paragraph:

> Since the major part of our time and our abilities is spent in work, for which we receive money, by offering to God part of our money we are, in fact, giving of Time, Abilities and Money.

This statement is an immediate offence against the true

principles of stewardship. The implication is that we are stewards only of that part of the money which we give away, perhaps even only that which passes through the church. That work itself is an ingredient of our religious life, which needs to be seen as part of our stewardship, would not suit the purposes of the argument at all, for the pamphlet is trying to urge people to give to the church. If the pamphlet was truly talking about Christian stewardship it would need to follow the phrase 'since the major part of our time and abilities is spent in work, for which we receive money' by saying something like 'then we should make certain that both our work and our money are brought under God's direction and rule'. The fact that it does not, demonstrates how right its readers are to treat the argument with some suspicion.

A little later, under a heading 'Balancing Your Budget', the pamphlet goes on:

> Having calculated what you would have to give to achieve the Diocesan Standard ... usually, to balance the budget, something will have to be reduced or even taken out. Should this be the contribution to God's work?

We must suppose from that statement that 'God's work' is to be found only within the activities that come within the purview of the church. To give your wife a bunch of flowers because it is her birthday or simply because you love her, to treat your husband to a new necktie, to send your children on an exchange visit to Germany, to buy saplings for the garden, books, new curtains, weekend break, second-hand car, hair-style or camera – all are outside God's work. This is absurd, of course, and as soon as it is spelt out it becomes obviously absurd. No sane Christian considers any of those items to be outside of God's care and responsibility. 'Put God first' says the pamphlet in capital letters, and if that meant that we were to bring the whole of our lives under the direction of God's will and to take infinite care over the way we allocate our resources then nobody could quarrel with it. But it does not. In the context the phrase 'Put God first' can only be interpreted as meaning 'Put God's work first', and by 'God's work' we have already been directed to our giving to and through the church. So by following the advice of the pamphlet we would not be putting God first. On the contrary, we would be squeezing him out into a corner labelled 'church' and permitting our lives outside the church to be at the direction of private whim. It is true that elsewhere in the pamphlet there is reference to 'other expenditure such as . . . Holidays, Hobbies, and Pastimes, Travel' about which we are encouraged to be 'honest and realistic', but only so that we can assess what I imagine the author of the pamphlet would consider to be 'secular expenditure' or some such phrase, and he remains unaware that the drift of the argument necessarily places these items outside 'God's work'.

For stewardship, as it is currently preached in the church, is not about our obligations to live the whole of our lives towards God but is essentially a way of seeking help for the church. This is further demonstrated by the way the pamphlet ends with a naked appeal to self-interest which no Christian would ever countenance in any field but this:

> Since all churches give to Missions and Charities, Christians should surely put their own Church first; and so most church members will want the greater part of their giving to go through the Church.

The rules of this kind of stewardship seem to be that the goal is to develop as widely as possible charitable giving to 'God's work', that is, the church, that this sort of giving is uniquely meritorious and that since Christian giving should be sacrificial (best represented in the phrase 'You must give till it hurts') it is seemly that Christians should be kept endlessly guilty about the level of their contributions. All this appears to me to be both a distortion of stewardship and calamitously un-Christian.

The Gospels are a much healthier guide. There we learn that riches of all kinds are extremely dangerous ('Be on your guard against greed of every kind', Luke 12.15), even worthless ('The things that are considered of great value by men are worth nothing in God's sight', Luke 16.15); that people who live by money will die by it (Parable of the Talents, Matt. 25.14–30) and it is better to be poor (Luke 6.20); that giving a tenth of our income does not justify us (The Pharisee and the Tax Collector, Luke 18.9–14), that we should learn to be thoughtlessly, eccentrically generous (The Widow's Offering, Mark 12.41–44), and that we can expect such generosity to be reciprocated in marvellous abundance ('Good measure pressed down, shaken together and running over will be poured into your lap', Luke 6.38); that we should quit fussing about it all ('How little faith you have!', Matt. 6.30) because it is God who makes things grow without our having to do anything about it (The Mustard Seed, Mark 4.26–29). St Paul sums it up well when he says that we should not give like a skeleton at the feast or because somebody is twisting our arm, for God loves 'a cheerful giver' (II Cor. 9.7 – the word 'cheerful' is a translation of a Greek word from which comes our word 'hilarity'). That gives something of the gospel spirit: 'God loves a hilarious giver'!

If we refuse to get caught up in that sort of manoeuvre we might well take some such action as this. The local church should be asked each year to produce a precise budget detailing the items of expected local expenditure, the amount claimed by central funds, sums likely to be needed for any capital expenditure such as major repairs to a building and the principles upon which the church deals with its responsibilities to the charitable and mission fields. We shall need to know in what way the local church expects to cover this budget and from what sources and by what means it intends to raise the money, ourselves endeavouring to assist in marshalling, where there is no such scheme, a method of sharing the costs fairly between the known members of the church. That will put us in possession of the data from church sources upon which a personal decision can be made.

Our next step is to turn to our own finances and to the allocation of our other resources of time and effort, concerning which we make an open and honest assessment in company with those in our family who share our responsibilities. It is crucial at this point that we keep the process of a consideration of our own resources quite separate from any claims the church may have upon us, for we are now reflecting on the obligations we owe to God, our stewardship before him and not before the church. Serious reflection at this point, informed by Bible, prayer and other teaching, could do all manner of things to our liberality and even to our manner and style of living itself. Only when we have completed that process before God do we turn to the claims of the church, decide how much of our resources it is right to offer to the church, give it peacefully and unostentatiously and turn our minds to other matters.

If we are on the other side of the fence, as fund-raisers, our duty is to refuse to allow the claims of the church to bear any undue weight. There are two realities which have to be presented to the members of the church: the claims of stewardship, which are claims that bite into the very centre of our lives, for they concern our attitude to those precious people and goods which we can scarcely bear to consider forsaking; and, separately, the needs of the church, which are important but transitory. These realities need to be sharply differentiated from one another and broached in quite unassociated contexts. To confuse them at any point leads inexorably to that besetting sin of the church, guilt-mongering.

Money seen as undermining faith

One of the main reasons why stewardship is so popular in the church is that it prevents us from having to face the issue of money head-on. If when we are talking about money we can pretend that it is not really money we are interested in but the whole shape of our lives before God we can attain several ends.

First, it does the job. Even our very short history of stewardship schemes shows that they work. The money comes in, people become engaged in church endeavours, central funds swell. The fact that the schemes have been, and still are, astonishingly successful is one of the main reasons why the church has not given more serious attention to the rationale behind them.

Secondly, it not only raises the money but does so under the camouflage of religious ends. As children grow they want to stay up later. 'None of my friends goes to bed at 7 o'clock', they say to their parents dismissively. They want to watch adult programmes on television, to stay out in the evening to play. Most of all they just want to be seen as more grown-up, and the later they can persuade their parents to permit them to stay up the more adult they appear. The parents are anxious that the children should not become over-tired. They worry about their homework, their readiness for school in the morning and whether they are going to become ill. It is a familiar battlefield, fought nearly always on the basis of the parents' anxieties for the children. 'Can't you see we are doing it for your own good', the parents bawl when tempers are roused. The level of the anger is an indication that other issues are at stake. For the children were once in bed and tucked up at 7 o'clock and the parents had the evening to themselves. The steady encroachment of the children upon their valuable time, perhaps the only time during the day that they had for each other, is a serious loss, a genuine sacrifice. Yet the battle is fought only on grounds of the parents' choosing. They say that their sole concern is for the children, and the children know, but cannot articulate, that the parents are more closely involved than that. The parents' solicitude for the children is real enough, but so are their fears about their personal loss, and the frustrated anger between parents and children is the result of a failure to face both issues honestly.

In some such way do we deceive ourselves about money and religion. We talk a great deal about God, commitment and sacrifice when we are raising funds because it feels less uncomfortable, more Christian, than talking about money directly. Certainly money is about God, but not quite in the way that we profess, and much of the strangled fury that money-talk raises in church circles is the result of this failure to be precise about the issues.

All of which leads to a recognition that stewardship campaigns are simply the outward manifestation of the Christian's constant fear that he or she might be appropriated by money. In face of all the frightening New Testament warnings, most of them from Jesus himself ('Fool! You are going to die tonight. Who will get your riches now?', Luke 12.20), we are wary of getting ourselves contaminated. We want to handle money with a long spoon, for money might take us over, draw us into the materialistic society, detach us from God.

We might imagine, then, a forum about church finance where at least one person present is directly involved as a benefactor in the chosen enquiry and another feels himself or herself to be responsible in some sense for the maintenance of religious purity. One party will be talking of budgets, targets, campaigns, balance sheets and cash, and the other will speak of commitment, service, prayer, opportunities and faith in God. The first party will suspect the second of being impractical and woolly-minded and the second believe the first to be insensitive and vulgar. Unless tempers are really roused, for instance through an inability to see any way to raise the money either by prayer or by campaigns, neither side is likely to voice their feelings about the other at the meeting because it would be felt to be unchristian to do so.

More usually the two sides of the argument war within us. When some kind of financial claim is laid upon us, we can hear both a religious and a vulgar voice speaking to us. The vulgar voice says that the church is always asking for money; we are pretty hard up at present but let's give them a cheque and get it over with, while the religious voice recalls how Jesus warned us against putting much store by riches and after all 'God so loved the world . . .'. Because we have been led to believe over the years that money really does undermine devotion and that the first voice might be the devil and the second God, we find ourselves frustrated whatever we do. 'Fool! . . .' and 'God so loved the world . . .' will not let us be satisfied this side of becoming a Franciscan monk, while to err on the side of parsimony leaves us feeling guilty and truculent.

Potential benefactors can make use of these uncertainties in order to slide away from their responsibilities. St Mark's church council decides that in their inner-city parish some action needs to be taken over the higher-than-average level of unemployment and suggest funding a resources centre for the unemployed. They make an appeal for £3,500 a year for three years and Mr Y, a member of the church council, agrees to approach Mrs J, a church member of some means who comes into worship from a further suburb. He puts his council's case and Mrs J replies, 'Yes, I'm sure it's a very good cause. It's a shame all those poor men not having any work. But do you think that it is something the church should do? Don't you think the church nowadays pays rather too much attention to money and money-raising? After all we are here to spread the gospel, aren't we? I think we ought to follow our Master more, don't you?' If Mr Y does not see the fallacy in the argument he leaves penniless and feeling either angry or depressed. Somehow he has been put in the wrong. The message is that the church is mercenary and has lost its true calling and that he himself is foolish and unspiritual. Mrs J comes out of it splendidly. Not only does she not have to relinquish one penny but she has turned the refusal into a pious act, reinforcing her own sense of godliness.

The subtlety is that Mrs J's arguments are so very nearly true. None but the wilfully blind can doubt the profound pressures upon men and women to fall in with a materialistic way of life that is so universally taken for granted. In the sense that the Christian, both as church and individual, is all the time insidiously tempted to judge the world by its own standards rather than by the religious requirement, money – above all money – does adulterate faith. But the way to control money is not to treat it as if it were an enemy or a weapon but to use it as an ally.

It yields best to a robust and level-headed realism. Some churches are very much better at this than others, and it is these churches which are doing no more than follow in the footsteps of St Paul whose considerable efforts at, and success with, fund-raising was never distorted by treating money either as God or as the devil. II Corinthians 9 shows a mingling of Christian theology with a straight appeal for money which stands as a matchless example of how it should be done.

The clue is to befriend money, to treat it like a well-worn garden spade, kept clean, polished and ready for the job in hand but otherwise hung up in the shed out of sight.

The pitfalls of generosity

Christians are encouraged to be generous to individuals as well as to the church. That seems to be a very simple, unexceptionable counsel. John comes back from work one day unexpectedly bringing his wife, Mary, a new handbag. Mary beams with delight. 'Oh John, you shouldn't!' she exclaims, 'and it exactly matches my blue outfit.' Next week he comes back with a bicycle for their son, Peter, and an enormous doll for Susan, their daughter. Peter and Susan feel terrific and give John a big hug. Mary is a little more confused. She is absolutely delighted for Peter and Susan and shares their excitement but she feels a touch of anxiety about John. She hugs him too but says, 'John, do you think we can afford it?' She is not wholly convinced by his reassurances and there may be another question lurking at the back of her mind, 'What is all this extravagant generosity about?'

Her fears are not put at rest when a fortnight later he brings her back a most beautiful and very expensive piece of jewellery. She no longer contains her anxieties. She challenges him directly about the cost and the purpose of these gifts. John is hurt. He has meant to bring happiness and is subjected to carping investigations, even anger. He replies that as a matter of fact he has also agreed to endow a bed at the local cottage hospital for their latest appeal. When Mary explodes he tells her huffily that whatever she thinks about it the local committee are very pleased and are going to make him a presentation.

Simple generosity has already turned into acrimony, fear, pique and blurred interaction. Let us briefly unpick some of the threads. We notice, for instance, that the destination of John's generosity is of great importance. Mary can bear John being generous within the family because she believes it to be in principle negotiable and she only explodes when she hears that he has independently committed his, that is the family's, resources to an outside body. The question, To whom is John meant to be generous? raises all the uncertainties about the boundaries of his responsibilities. Where should he stop? Generosity will normally make people happy; but not everybody, and others will react with contrary emotions. The cottage hospital fundraisers are very pleased but Mary hits the roof. Peter and Susan hug John delightedly, Mary with less warmth. Gratitude is simplest where there is least understanding of the possible implications of the donor's act. Mary wants and needs to protect the family, and she also needs to understand what lies behind the shift in John's behaviour. To give bountifully and unexpectedly can imply a secret windfall or it may mean that one partner desires, probably unconsciously, to exert pressure in the family, to demonstrate where strength really belongs and therefore who is the weaker. Such a challenge needs to be opposed because only so can the balance in the relationship be discovered, agreed and maintained. To accept humiliation is an excellent test of the soul on occasions but is scarcely a recipe for a satisfying marriage. And what would happen between them, Mary reflects, if she were to go out and buy John a new workbench and tools? Or herself a new washing machine?

The pitfalls of generosity do not take much discerning and the chances are that John's motives would bear some closer examination. In any incident where one person is the giver and the other the recipient it may be implied that the giver possesses both the means and the qualities to be generous and the recipient has neither. The giver is therefore superior, and the payoff concluding any transaction is the self-satisfied smirk on the face of the donor and a feeling of impotence in the receiver.

The point is nicely illustrated in the hoary but delightful tale of the tramp who called one day at a private home and asked the lady of the house if she could spare him something to eat. Saying, 'Wait there', she shut the door and went off into the kitchen, returning a few minutes later with a hunk of dry bread and a small piece of cheese. She gave them to him with the words, 'Of course you understand, my man, that I am giving you this for God's sake.' The tramp looked at the offering, reflected for a moment and then said, 'Well, for Christ's sake put some butter on it!' The ruse is observed, assessed and in one telling phrase demolished.

Political creeds have been and still are passionately created and espoused on the basis of the need for generosity or its antithesis so it is not surprising that Christians should also be heavily involved in this well-documented type of behaviour. In many forms it is universally despised in the church. People smile at the old-fashioned picture of the minister's wife and her large-hatted partners ladling out soup to the poor. 'Lady Bountiful' has become a derogatory term. Charitable societies which deal in overseas relief go to exceptional lengths to ensure that the recipient churches have full autonomy over the dispersion of their gifts. All of which is not to say that people do not display similar behaviour in more subtle forms.

Attempts are still made to buy, if not nowadays salvation, at least self-satisfaction, for cash. Mrs J of St Mark's referred to in the last section may choose to play with her possession of money not by refusing to give it and justifying her refusal as a pious act but by promising it and using her generosity as a means of manipulation. When Mr Y calls she is full of funds for the moment and is looking for something to occupy her mind. So when the proposition is put to her she is interested and asks all about it. However, she is unsatisfied and questions Mr Y about detail he is unable to supply, so she sends him back to the council to get further information. When he returns she says that she thinks she ought to come and talk to the minister, and after an afternoon with him requests a meeting with the full council. She has by now established herself as a major potential benefactor of the new scheme and has the whole church council waiting for her decision. It is a position of some power, and she may choose to make the very best of it for quite some time, and even then, in a triumphant *coup de main*, revert to her previous stratagem and say that she does not think that the church council has its priorities quite right and regretfully she feels she must decline to contribute. If she does make a benefaction she can continue to maintain a delightful hold upon the council for a considerable time by fussily demanding to be kept fully informed of progress, interfering in the detail and using her generosity as a means of bending the scheme in the way she chooses.

There are, as usual, only shades of difference between Mrs J's behaviour and the action of any responsible subscriber. Anybody should take good care to see that their money is being spent wisely, should ask for details, see whomever they wish, decline to give if they choose and make suggestions as the scheme progresses. But there is one unerring way by which it may be told whether the concern is genuine or not and that is by the level of frustration in the other members of the church. There is always a direct correlation between the attitude adopted and the level of feelings of impatience aroused. A majority of church members will be able to distinguish unhesitatingly between genuine concern and manipulation, and their feelings are almost always to be trusted.

I have recently come across a more sophisticated way of using generosity for one's own purposes. Two companions were sharing a home together, surviving deliberately at a very frugal standard of living. At Christmastime, however, they always had a feast and one of them rang a close friend of theirs to ask if he would buy a bottle of wine and bring it with him when he came. The understanding was unspoken but quite clear between them that they were to pay for the wine. When the friend arrived and gave them the wine they had the money ready and offered it to him. He said, 'Oh, don't bother about that. Accept it as a gift.' One of them said that was 'embarrassing' but the friend shrugged it off.

During the day he pondered on what he had done and did not much like what he saw, so he said in due course, 'I'm sorry, I don't think I should have given you that wine. I think I should have taken your money. Somehow, in a way I can't quite put my finger on, making it a gift like that has inhibited and demeaned you.' One of the companions grinned widely at him. 'Do you know,' he said, 'I think you are the first person we have ever known to see that.'

Thinking and talking about it afterwards they all saw that on the surface there was no harm in the world in what the friend had done. They were poor and he was, relatively, rich. He was fond of them and chose to express his affection by turning their request into a gift. What possible damage could come of a kindness like that?

Much every way. In the first place he had made it very difficult for them to ask him to go shopping for them ever again because he might act in just the same way and offer the goods to them as a gift. That would again be, as one of them described it, 'embarrassing', because it might easily look as if every future request of theirs was a covert appeal for aid. He would not know whether that was the case or not. He might have sufficient trust in his friends not to suspect them of it, but a series of requests could begin to throw some doubt upon their motives and produce some irritation in him. He could not know whether they were genuinely needing to take advantage of his generosity and he certainly would not wish them to go hungry, but they would not want to make an unwarranted imposition on his generosity nor would they wish to put themselves in the position of being beggars. None of these doubts could comfortably be brought out into the open and this incapacity could be the beginning of a distance, an unease, between them.

He had, moreover, created a worse sort of distance than that, for he had taken all initiative right out of their hands. If he had taken them a bottle of wine for Christmas as a gift that would have been fine. But since he had given them a bottle which they had requested he had put himself irretrievably in the position of a benefactor who had been not just generous but had gone further than was asked of him. He was conspicuously warm-hearted, an example of Christian philanthropy which they were in no position to reciprocate. A part of him was using the two companions as an instrument for his self-satisfaction.

To the uninvolved spectator that story may appear ludicrous. The ordinary person in each of us wants to say, 'Are we not permitted then to be kind to our indigent friends?' And of course we may. As I have tried to show earlier in this chapter, loving generosity is of the essence of the gospel. But it is not for the outsider to judge what manner of generosity is being offered. The participants' feelings are the ones to be trusted, and the relieved smile on the face of one of the companions when the friend expressed his hesitations about his action was the clearest of recognitions that the game had been properly identified. The companion knew he was being used but could not say so for fear of upsetting his friend by throwing doubts upon his motives, and at the same time making himself appear touchy.

If we do not wish to compromise the integrity of those with whom we wish to share our good fortune we would be well-advised to clear the air with the recipients first, as these three friends eventually came to identify and acknowledge the choices they had made with their lives and unhurriedly to bargain their way through to some frank agreements.

4 | The Believer and the Minister

I now turn to the questions inherent in maintaining or serving authority. It is a dilemma for the whole world. Who should be in charge? Who appears to be in charge? Who is in fact in charge? What does, or should, happen when two or more co-equal authorities claim command of the same possession? How obedient should subjects be? What rights do subjects have? What should subjects do when faced with substantive but conflicting authorities? To what degree, if any, may subjects resist authority? What sanctions may authorities apply to enforce obedience?

Relate questions like these to the family (parents v. children), to the factory (management v. workers), to the school (teachers v. students), to the nation (government v. people) or to the international scene (one nation v. another) and we at once bring a hornet's nest of prejudice and opinion, of passion and triumph, buzzing about our ears. Add to these, specifically religious questions like: Is obedience compatible with love? Can it be right for those who call themselves brothers and sisters to practise obedience? What is the meaning of becoming 'like children' in order to enter the kingdom of God? Is democracy better than a Pope? What do we mean by talking of God's authority? and the wonder is that there is not a fury of discussion in the church about the nature of authority.

In practice there is plenty of fury but little discussion, and much of both the fury and the discussion is veiled. The discussion, where it occurs, is conducted more often in terms of loyalty and obedience than of the claims of freedom and love, and people become angry but gagged because they are tacitly discouraged from pursuing an enquiry which might appear unfilial. Church authority uses the reluctance of ordinary Christians to express their negative feelings openly (because it is 'not Christian') to stifle a wide-ranging debate which could throw doubt upon traditional perceptions of their office. So discussion becomes muted in emotion and in range.

It is essential, for the very survival of the human race, let alone its adherence to the religious quest, that the church should be in the vanguard of the discussion about the nature of authority because it relates so closely to the substance of humanity. As one possible point of departure for such a discussion I shall begin by referring to a famous experiment conducted about twenty years ago by one Stanley Milgram at Yale University in the United States, an experiment that was subsequently repeated in other countries with very similar results. The details that follow may be found in H. and M. Eysenck's *Mindwatching*.*

Milgram, over a period of three years, set up a series of experiments to try and discover how far ordinary people are prepared to be obedient to an outside authority to which they are not bound by ties of loyalty. He created a laboratory in which there were two rooms, invisible to each other but joined by sound equipment. In one of the rooms there was an electric chair apparatus into which a person could be strapped. Electrodes attached to such a person's wrist could then be connected to a shock generator unit which was in the other room. This unit could administer electric shocks from 15 to 450 volts, ranging from slight shock to severe shock, and there were two final switches simply marked XXX.

A 'learner' (who was in fact Milgram's stooge) was strapped into the electric chair in front of a 'teacher', who was one of a series of the subjects of the experiment. The teacher was then taken into the room that contained the shock generator unit and was asked to put a series of questions to the learner which, if he failed to answer, he, the teacher, was to administer a low level shock, gradually increasing the voltage. The teacher was told that it was an experiment in the effects of punishment upon learning. The learner, who was not of course actually receiving any shocks at all, though the teacher

* H. and M. Eysenck, *Mindwatching*, Michael Joseph 1981, pp. 35–41.

did not know this, began by grunting after receiving the lower voltage shocks when he was unable to answer a question, moved to cries of 'Stop!' and by 270 volts was screaming. If the teacher at any time expressed a desire to stop the experiment Milgram told him that he had to go on.

The appalling result of this experiment was that sixty-two per cent of a random selection of men and women were prepared to obey the experimenter and administer shocks to the learner to the maximum 450-volt level, very nearly a fatal dose. There were naturally many signs of extreme tension in the teachers during the experiment. One 'pushed his fist into his forehead and muttered, "Oh God, let's stop it". And yet he continued to respond to every word of the experimenter, and obeyed to the end.' Another woman who did volunteer work with juvenile delinquents and was active in the local Girl Scout organization indignantly said that she would certainly need no more than fifteen volts, if that, to help her as a learner, yet as a teacher was prepared to administer to somebody else the maximum 450-volt shock. There was no difference in the results between male and female teachers, and similar experiments in Rome, South Africa, Australia and Munich have shown levels of obedience greater than Milgram obtained in the USA.

Milgram was an impersonal experimenter. Though he wore a doctor's white coat and practised with the authority of Yale University behind him, the subjects of the experiment owed him no kind of personal loyalty. If a random collection of ordinary human beings reacted to that sort of authority with such merciless obedience, it is deeply worrying to reflect how much worse things might be when close personal ties are added to the equation. Milgram's research lends a sombre background to what follows.

The minister as parent

It was a couple of days before Christmas. I was fairly busy at the time and we were expecting fifteen people for lunch on Christmas Day, so there was a certain amount of tension domestically as well. My son, just nine years old, was slouching about the house, not helping much, so I asked him to go and buy something for us at the shops. He complained bitterly and I, my anger erupting, shouted at him and he shouted back. He then retired to his bedroom, sulking, where five minutes later I visited him and asked him quietly to go to the shops. He went off and I retired to my study. After he had come back with the shopping he knocked on my door, came in and glared at me. He said, 'Do you want me to call you Merciful Lord next?', turned and left.

That incident, related with his consent, was one of the seedbeds in the growth of my understanding of the perils of authority, and it was no coincidence that it arose in a parent/child conflict. There is a proper expectation in a family that all its members take some part in its organization and most people will agree that it was quite reasonable that I as a parent should have attempted to enforce the participation of my son. Most of the time he himself accepts that he has responsibilities and carries them out voluntarily. He accepts, too, that parents have a duty of enforcement, though his 'natural man' will resist it when he can. Thus part of his remark was simply to let me know that he knew I was boss, that he resented it but he complied nevertheless. Open acknowledgement of power is better than silent resentment of it. My anger did not matter so much because it was a testimony to his strength. He was able to match my anger and that made us quits.

Why 'Merciful Lord' though? I believe that was a reference to my second meeting with him when I had calmed down, went to visit him in his bedroom and silkily invited him to fall in with my wishes. There my power was being exhibited in a different form. I was now the bearer of reconciliation, the good parent who forgave his son's unreasonable temper – and yet was still demanding obedience. This was a total undermining of his position, because I was still 'Lord', but was now also 'Merciful', and to resist forbearance is doubly blameworthy. So his remark to me, within the realities of power between us, was a restoration of equivalence.

As I have said, few will deny the right, indeed the positive duty, of parents to attempt to keep defining the boundaries within which the family shall operate. Since I have (at the moment!) more power than my son and since I have an obligation to bring him up with what I believe to be well-founded ideas about co-operation and mutual forgiveness, the action I took was in principle defensible, even if in practice deficient.

The truth we now have to face in this context is that such a relationship does not exist between adults. No adult, unless he chooses to create one, has any father save the one from whose loins he or she came. As adults we meet other authorities which have some rightful dominion over us, like school teachers, the police and government departments. We are bound to go to school, to obey the law and to pay our taxes with the threat of sanctions if we do not. But these authorities do not exercise paternal rights over us unless we choose to concede them.

Yet there is a strong tendency in humankind to repeat with all other authorities the patterns of its parental relationships, particularly if, and where, those relationships have been unfulfilling. There is nothing strange about this. Most of us live with our parents for a fair number of years and those the most impressionable. Parents are the first authorities we know, and we are bound to use them as models (not necessarily in the sense that we model ourselves on them, rather that they are the prototypes by which we judge subsequent authorities). It is not in the least surprising, therefore, if for example, a man meets an obstinate policeman and reacts with the cowed sullenness he always displayed with his father or the vindictive abuse he always wanted to deal out but rarely dared. Children who never received the parental care they required may make heavy demands upon teachers at school and as adults become easily dependent upon anybody who shows kindness, the dependence being displayed initially in the expected subservience and then in anger whenever they are deprived of what they consider their proper due. The adult becomes locked in a framework where he or she not only resists what is conceived to be the malign control of the authority but is also beguiled by, and therefore frustrated by, that authority's benevolence, just as my son was.

If we now turn that situation back to front, it at once becomes obvious how tempting it is for authorities of all kinds to respond to such advances with relish. He who is addressed 'Merciful Lord' becomes a merciful Lord. It gratifies us when people look up to us, rely upon us, seek our advice, treat us as somebody to be reckoned

with. We all seek recognition one way or another and esteem is one
of the most pleasurable. It is no less welcome when we are seen as
a pernicious authority, provided we are sure of the grounds of our
control. For aggression is a sure sign that we are important to the
aggressor, and in the absence of aggression we have all the blandish-
ments of naked power. Once we defer, however, to those who wish
us to exercise paternal rights over them; when, that is, we permit
ourselves to be treated as a parent, we immediately become bonded
into the disequilibrium which belongs in the first instance to them
and not to us. Only in the first instance, though, for we have had
parents of our own who have lent us a greater or a lesser balance,
and the affiliation of our 'son' becomes intertwined with our own
parenting, creating a tangle which at times is wholly confusing.
We have run ourselves into a trap where the other is already in
residence. We cannot love him satisfactorily nor, except within the
narrow confines of our professional expertise, can we offer him
any real assistance. We are still 'parent' to him and not an autonomous human being, so we are unable to separate ourselves from
him in any bid he might make for independence.

Any kind of authority then may draw out of us, usually unwittingly, a parent/child response. Politicians, government officials,
teachers and similar bearers of lawful authority claim some kind of
hegemony over us and we play the child to them to the extent that
we have or have not worked through our childhood dependence.
Or on the other side of the equation we may take the part of the
parent-authority ourselves, and it is this behaviour that I now want
to examine in the context of the minister and congregation.

The case may be introduced with the trenchant words of Clifford
Longley, religious affairs correspondent of *The Times* newspaper.
In 1978 he noted that a group of distinguished, liberal German
theologians had petitioned the conclave of Roman Catholic cardi-
nals who were shortly to meet to choose a new Pope. The Pope,
they said, need not be a saint but should reflect the contemporary
age in several ways they went on to catalogue, the details of which
do not concern us here. Mr Longley took up the implications of
their position in an article printed on 21 August that year. He
wrote:

It is fair comment to ask whether it is a healthy and realistic premise for the Roman Catholic Church that only an uncanonized saint would be good enough for the top job. If that is the logic of the situation, then there must be something wrong with it . . . Pope Paul saw himself as a parish priest with the whole world as his parish. It is a comforting image; somewhere a father figure cared about every human life everywhere, wished to ease the burden of life from mankind and to place it upon his own shoulders. It corresponds to the almost universal desire to escape back to the security of childhood, where important decisions can be left trustingly in the hands of all-wise, all-knowing parents. It is the benign face of patriarchy; the image of the church, or the whole human race, as a family with a father. The demand for a progressive, or even permissive, father, in essence the demand of the theologians, is the common demand of adolescence. As all fathers of all adolescents know, it is a demand fraught with contradictions . . . The church was not founded as a community of dependent children, but as a brotherhood of adults . . . it is only through brotherhood that the fatherhood of God can be at all apprehended. Father figures are dangerous; anyone searching for a 'father' has to be referred not to Rome but to heaven, and to accept the uncomfortable consequences.

If a Pope is a minister writ large, what Mr Longley says about him applies to many ministers, too. The temptations are great. Ministers practise the only profession in the world where a man is able to talk without fear of contradiction or interruption for as long as he likes. They claim mystic spheres of authority from which, in many cases, everybody else is excluded unless they have undergone long training and special rites. The gospel they preach they assert to be 'true' in an exclusive sense and they seal it with the authority of the Holy Trinity. Whatever view is taken of their testimony, it cannot be surprising if it sometimes goes to their heads, and all of us can call to mind examples of people who have become, without ever intending it, arrogant in the service of their master.

Many more, however, feeling the weight of their calling, only with great diffidence make their strenuous efforts to live up to it.

They discipline themselves, doggedly bear all manner of disappointments, refuse the easy paths, make themselves all things to all people. They aim for perfection because it is what they demand of themselves and what people expect of them. When perfection eludes them, as it eludes all of us, a practical method of resolving the resulting tension is to split off that which belongs to the office from that which belongs to the person. 'The minister' and 'John Smith' become separate people. Mothers will often do the same sort of thing with their children. They will say, 'Now Mummy is going down to the shops so don't get into any mischief while she's away', or, 'That wasn't a very nice thing to do to Mummy, was it?' In this way they create an image of motherhood. The child is faced not with Jane or Lilian who happens to be their mother and who can be identified and engaged, but with an indeterminate member of the mother-tribe called 'Mummy' who, under pressure, retreats behind her office where she is protected from personal assaults and from having to confront her own strengths and inadequacies. Similarly, ministers may make a 'fatherhood' for themselves (which they sometimes identify openly in those terms) because in that way they can give some protection to the purity of the gospel at the same time as they concede their own limitations.

Once the procedure is recognized, it is not difficult to call to mind circumstances in which we practise it. Some ministers use it as a means of getting their own way and of maintaining their superiority. Flowers on the altar table, statues in the church's niches and gospel campaigns in the local area are the small change of such transactions with the minister's petulant, 'You are all so un-christian!' when he is challenged. More dangerous are the *ex cathedra* statements of gospel truth ('This is what you are to believe'), instructions disguised as advice and the assumption of control over the direction of people's lives. More often it is less blatant, kinder. Avuncular is the word that leaps to mind. Dominance is maintained by a display of such unmistakable affability that it is an obvious offence to oppose it.

So deep-seated are many of these attitudes and so circumstantially determined that some damage can be caused if we make ham-handed attempts to counteract them. Nor is it ever quite clear how

far we ourselves are involved on one or the other – or both – sides
of the game! It is not that some of us are stuck in a parental authority framework and some of us are free from it; for all of us it is a
question of degree. None of us escapes completely, or indeed
legitimately, from the influence of our parents, yet we do need
some measure of detachment. Perhaps one of the most helpful
ways forward is to make some attempt to come to terms with our
own needs.

And at once, where ministers are concerned, we are faced with
some incredulity. It is not always apparent to an outsider that
ministers have, or in any case should have, any personal or spiritual
needs, and not always clear to either the outsider or the ministers
themselves that it would be at all appropriate to speak of them if
they had. On the contrary, ministers are often seen to be possessed
by God in a fashion denied to the layman and of having a vocation
to fulfil the needs of others rather than of sharing their own. To
many people it still remains a slightly absurd fancy that ministers
need to be looked after in the same way as they strive to care for
others, and ministers themselves may compound the problem by
feeling in their turn that they ought to lead their people with a
strength of conviction and a personal heroism which shows an
example to everybody, so that any hint (apart from the generally
admissible 'we all fall short of the glory of God') that they themselves have any real, personal needs could weaken the basis of the
faith itself. The minister is a sort of bastion against unfaith.

This places a burden upon ministers which is both heavy and
unreal, heavy because the expectations laid upon them become too
high, and unreal because the slightest scratching beneath the surface demonstrates that ministers share the doubts, failures and
disappointments of their congregations and need to receive their
love and encouragement quite as much as they are happy to give
such support. For ministers humanly to isolate themselves from
the congregation creates the very fragility they are striving to avoid.
The barriers between them become the ideals that ministers think
they ought to, and the people know they cannot, achieve.

When ministers can bring themselves to admit that they have
needs and to state what they are, a reciprocity flows through the

church. People begin to see at last that none of us can save ourselves, that we need each other's faith and love, that there is
enough to do together and to learn from each other without en-
cumbering ourselves with unattainable ideals. Within that atmosphere it becomes possible to recognize our needs for ascendancy
and for dependence and so to embark upon a discovery of inte-
grated living. In this way the need to be or to suffer a parental
authority diminishes day by day.

Sharing authority

The modern church has discovered 'the people'. It could scarcely
have done otherwise in an era which is becoming more self-
consciously autonomous all the time. 'The people of God', 'the
church is the people', 'the church family' – these are the common-
places of today.

In the Church of England the process started with the 1919
Enabling Act which instituted mandatory church councils and
ancillary democratic bodies, thus giving the laity as a whole, and
not just those ancient officers, the churchwardens, a formal voice
in the church's affairs. The people were now there, in the popular
phrase, 'to help the clergy in their work', and many of them took
up their task with a willing grace. A development of that initiative
arrived with the 1968 Pastoral Measure in which co-operation between the minister and the people was the watchword. Church
affairs now became, by statute, an exercise carried out by the
minister and people jointly rather than the latter giving assistance
to the former, and various safeguards were instituted for each
party. Doubtless a similar pattern of burgeoning democracy has
taken place in those other churches which have a long history of
clericalism.

Ministers have found the process a mixed blessing. They have
found it helpful to have much of the drudgery of the day-to-day
affairs of the church taken off their shoulders and no longer to be
automatically at the apex of every church function. Many ministers
are rightly proud of their laity-led schemes of Bible-study, home
visiting, magazine editing and suchlike. But there comes a point

at which so much is done by the laity that it can throw doubt upon what the minister's role might be, and it is at this point that ministers begin hedging with unspoken conditions the release of their authority.

An elderly lady, for instance, who has been teaching the young children of the church for some years resigns and a replacement has to be found. The minister talks to the church council about it. He tells them that in the modern church every member has to take some responsibility. It is a part of the new understanding of the nature of the church that the minister and people now share the responsibility. He looks around upon them severely and they shuffle in their seats hoping that his eye is not upon them. (There is often a subtle expectation within church councils and similar bodies that the response to requests for help must come from those who have been kind and bold enough to stand for election in the first place.) Nobody volunteers, however, and at the end of the meeting the minister adds a twist to the screw of rising guilt by including in his closing prayers a request that the right person may come forward. At this point he feels, and the church council makes no attempt to relieve, full responsibility for discovering a new volunteer.

After a week or two during which the church leaders have been busy, rumours reach the minister's ear that Mr L, who is not on the council, might be persuaded to take the job on. He visits Mr L and persuades him to give it a try. He then hands over to Mr L the book that the retiring teacher has been using, says that he hopes he will be able to start in the new year, and if he is in any trouble is not to hesitate to come and talk it over with him.

At this stage we should pause to note how responsibility for the task has been passed from retiring teacher to minister to Mr L but that responsibility within the task has not been talked about at all. Mr L has very little to go on except his native wit. He does not know whether the council has planned a strategy with respect to the younger members of the church and whether he is expected to continue teaching in the same way as, and with the same book as, the retiring teacher. He has been offered no access to the council and only an informal one to the minister. He goes along to see the retiring teacher to find out some of the background and decides in his own way that he would like to make one or two modest changes.

A fortnight before he is due to begin the minister calls bringing a new teaching book. Now that there is a change in the leadership, he says, he would like to take the opportunity of moving things along and he would be most grateful if Mr L would give the book a trial. The book does not really suit Mr L's style and he has not been offered much time but out of loyalty he agrees to experiment with it. He is under some pressure, therefore, in the first couple of sessions of the new term, getting to know the children, labouring with the unfamiliar book and trying out his experiments, and he is surprised and embarrassed when the minister arrives unexpectedly at the third session when discipline has momentarily broken down. He sees the frown on the minister's face and hurries to explain. He has decided, he says, not to gather the children to opening worship every Sunday because he would value them working in small groups for the full hour. As the minister can see, he adds, things have not quite settled down yet. The minister replies firmly that he is sure Mr L's intentions are good but he really must insist on an act of worship every Sunday and he explains why at some length. Perhaps it would be a good idea, he finishes with a tight smile, if he himself came in once a month to give some assistance.

It is not necessary to labour the story further. We are already aware of the mounting confusion and irritation in Mr L and can see that he will soon either blow his top, or capitulate or resign his new office. The minister is giving him an inch but is making quite sure that he will not take a mile. On the other hand, whatever Mr L does, the minister is now going to find himself in a tangle. If Mr L resigns, the responsibility for finding someone else to take his place is going to fall back upon the minister, particularly since it is his remarks which have caused the resignation. He does not want that to happen and will therefore make some attempt to appease Mr L, an attitude which he feels angry at having to adopt and which immediately undermines any possibility of a mature relationship. He wants to avoid a row because, as usual, rows are seen to be un-Christian. He will therefore have to embark upon an equivocal relationship with Mr L. He will have to go as far as he dares in urging Mr L to fall in with some of the practices and teaching content which he feels bound to insist on because he is answerable to God, while Mr L on his side will need to defend enough of his initiatives to feel that he is making a personal contribution. Between them will lie a no-man's land which will be the arena of all their future misunderstandings.

In the world of industry we hear about demarcation disputes and we laugh when we are told that management has to call in an electrician to change a light bulb. The seriousness with which such issues are treated, however, bears witness to the universal demand for a precise definition of responsibility. In the church job definition is normally blurred, and additionally confused by the fact that the vast majority of those who participate do so voluntarily. It is right that the trained minister should have some say in what and how the children of the church should be taught but not clear how much authority the willing but possible untrained church member has. In all such cases, since there is no adjudicator, it is up to the participants to come to some agreed definition of the authority each bears and, once they are defined as accurately as the situation allows, to permit each person autonomy within his own sphere of responsibility, subject to regular reappraisal. In our example the church council would itself engage itself seriously in a discussion of what they believed should take place in the teaching of the young and how they expected to achieve it and would openly share the responsibility of filling the vacant post. The minister would relinquish both the burden and the sole control of choosing a new person. He would make clear to the new appointee what he and the church would like to see done and compare it with what the appointee would like to do, coming to some agreed compromise about it. The new leader would not fail to challenge the minister, and through him the council, about their perceptions of the job.

The interaction could take an even more destructive turn. The minister would make a good show of having a discussion with Mr L over the content of the job and would come to an apparent agreement with him, but then, at the point when anything arose to disturb him, would establish his ascendancy ruthlessly by saying that he had been good enough to have a full discussion with Mr L before he took the job on and really he cannot be responsible for every little upset that happens; perhaps Mr L should examine again the methods he himself insisted on adopting. Any mistake made by the minister could be laid at the door of Mr L who would have been drawn into a collusion by the display of consultation. Or Mr L could play a similar game by remarking coldly that if only the minister had not insisted on interfering so much this trouble would never have happened. But these sorts of manoeuvres lead us into the final section of this chapter.

Consultation as a means of control

The theme of this final section still concerns shared, or apparently shared, areas of responsibility and how, and within what limits, authority is exercised there but differs in three ways from the behaviour we have just been examining.

First, we are talking of situations in which the ingredient of decision-making is normally a good deal stronger. The minister and Mr L had a task to perform over a long period; here, there is more often than not a clear once-for-all decision to be made. Secondly, because decisions are usually taken by those in charge and more senior people more frequently make decisions, this device is a regular feature at management level but is less common in any but the larger local churches. The most significant difference, however, is that here the participants have a predetermined intention (though it sometimes acts at an unconscious level) to keep control in their hands. Because the decision is to be made evidentially and the decision-makers are most commonly absent from the scene of its effects, they are able to implement their plans without undue hindrance.

Consultation is widespread throughout the Western world, might almost be said to have reached the stage of an epidemic: not a government department, not a trade union, not a pressure group or church but what holds a consultation or establishes consultative

procedures or forms a consultative body or simply consults the
people. Everybody expects to be consulted about matters close to
their heart and will react with spirited indignation if they are not.
Far fewer have given serious consideration to how consultation
might relate to the realities of power, and it is sometimes authori-
tarianism which, without conscious duplicity, slips into the gap.

Let us return to our district church official who was, you may
recall, working for a Gaussian victory (see p. 26). He had been
deputed by the district church committee to visit a church which
had decreased in membership from fifty to twenty-three members
and to tell them that they would have to close. This time he has
been asked not to help the committee to come to terms with a
decision already made but to 'consult' them. The facts are the
same. The church is too small to be viable and will have to go, but
this time they say to one another, 'We must consult the people.
You go and talk to them. Let them see all the facts. Let them face
the realities.'

With this brief the district church official visits the church one
evening and has, it must be admitted, a rather more candid evening
than the one previously described. He is open and honest. He tells
them that he is not there to pull the wool over their eyes; they can
read the facts like anybody else, and he spends some time going
over the arguments for closure. 'What other solution can there be?',
he ends. The people slowly begin to make their response, talking
of the warm friendliness of the church and the sadness of breaking
the fellowship, yet they have an instinct that the horse has already
bolted. The official, well practised in consultative procedures,
agrees wholeheartedly with all their positive statements. He tells
them, 'From all quarters we hear how faithful you are and the
district council was only saying the same thing this week.' After
some further discussion he smiles, gathers his papers and departs,
congratulating himself on the way the meeting has gone. The
people return home, grateful for a chance to talk but sensing their
powerlessness.

The church members, however, have not been offered a consultation which has any chance of being effective. On the contrary,
they have been emasculated. At worst it may have been a cynical

device of the district committee to manipulate the church members and to muffle dissent. Having made its decision, the committee is determined to gain its objective with as little fuss as possible and send the official to make a conscious attempt to disarm them and render their unavoidable protests harmless. A pre-emptive strike, as the army puts it. At best they may have had little understanding of the nature of power and thought that they were making a genuine consultation. Most times it lies somewhere in between the two extremes, any reservations about the process being tacitly suppressed.

Note how those who most frequently seek a consultation in this form never force a confrontation, because that gives the conflict a prominence they are trying to avoid. The official was not foolish enough to argue with the church members when they claimed their fellowship was valuable to them. On the contrary he agreed with all they had to say. He even set the district council's seal of approval on their friendliness. This made them impotent because it invalidated the only argument the church possessed. If the district council has already so fully taken into account what the church members feel, it renders the church's position feeble and the council's impregnable.

To make a valid consultation, everything depends upon the stage at which it takes place. And that in its turn depends upon the beliefs of those who possess power about the value of those over whom they wield it and about the extent to which they are prepared to share it. The realities of the situation where a declining church is in view cannot be gainsaid. The district church council has responsibility for the disposition of its ministers, for some financial control of the area and for making and putting into effect fruitful, wide-ranging policies. They fail in their duties if they do not carry out these functions. On the other hand they do not exercise their powers in isolation. They are dependent upon the local churches because without them they themselves will cease to exist, and the local churches have definite and interlocking powers of their own. The local church is in possession of the buildings and cares for them, it supports its part-time minister and contributes towards the salaries of the very officials who are now planning its obsolescence. It has the power of its solidarity, of its faith, of its traditions and memories. These powers are all weaker, less decisive, than those of the council, but they are real enough and a wise council will not act as if they are of no account.

So a genuine consultation will take place *before* any binding decision is made, thereby giving a chance for the weaker power to contribute towards the discussion rather than accept a decision already made. That sounds easy enough. In practice it is a good deal harder than it looks. The district committee is bound to do some thinking beforehand, otherwise there will be nothing to discuss and no facts upon which to base a discussion. They might even be driven towards some initial ideas about policies. The difficulty comes in choosing the moment to consult before those first thoughts congeal into hardened policies. The clue is in general to seek to consult as early as possible in the discussion consonant with the possibility of a coherent exchange of views. To do this the hierarchy has to be fully convinced that the lesser power is worth consulting and might have approaches of its own which will shift the discussion into another plane. There is, of course, a strong reluctance to make such an early approach because it is disturbing to the primary authority's routine and its own self-image.

To ensure that consultation takes place early enough is one way of doing what Richard Sennett, in a stimulating book entitled *Authority*, calls 'disrupting the chain of command' in order to prevent a hierarchy becoming either compulsively paternalistic or loftily autonomous, yet without inhibiting effective government. Another way he suggests is 'to require the use of the active voice in the chain of command' in order to do 'the work of making authority work'. He quotes, for example, a notice pinned on the board of an industrial concern about summer holidays for the workers, couched in highly bureaucratic language. 'It has been decided that employees will have to sequence their vacations over the entire summer period. Thus it will be necessary for each employee to file . . . These will then be co-ordinated by the supervisory groups and a vacation schedule will be assigned each employee.' Sennett rewrites that order in the active voice:

Mrs Jones, Mr Smith, Mr Anderston and Miss Barker decided to tell employees when they could take their vacations this summer. The reason is that the productivity of the organization is disrupted if everyone is away in August. Jones, Smith and Barker voted for this decision, Anderston voted against, saying that the time necessary to co-ordinate the vacations of a thousand employees would cost the company as much money in the end as letting them determine in each department when they will be away.*

Direct, personal speech is a beautifully simple but very exacting way of making an honest match between collective and individual responsibility.

A third way is to take as few decisions as possible at the top and to leave broad areas for local decision. If the district church committee is brought reluctantly to the conclusion that for financial and personnel reasons half a dozen churches in their district have to close, they are not bound to go on and say which churches those shall be. They could as well say to the whole district or to smaller areas of it, 'It seems to us that we will have to make some adjustments in the area. We cannot afford so many buildings and ministers. In order to keep within our budget half a dozen or so will have to go. Here are the figures for you to examine. Perhaps you would now like to talk between yourselves as to what you think should happen and which church, if any, should close.'

The district council has now made moves within its own sphere of competence and is leaving the rest of the church an area for manoeuvre. There will not now be antagonism between an upper and a lower authority, nor can the lower authority any longer project all its anger at the necessary closures back on to their superiors. They have to make their own decisions, healthily fighting it out with their peers. If the suggested scheme does not find universal approval in the group, then it remains their task to find another that does. They can no longer slough off their responsibility and say, 'Look what a wicked father/authority is making us do.' Provided that their conclusions are not wildly inappropriate (which is

* Richard Sennett, *Authority*, Secker and Warburg 1980, p. 180.

always the fear of all hierarchies and their excuse for not adopting this procedure) the purposes of all the participants have been achieved without a single person being rendered impotent.

5 | The Believer with other Believers

Some of the most poignant and damaging inventions of all are those which Christians practise on one another. We can often distance ourselves far enough from the church as an organization and from its ministers to laugh at them, or at least not to take them as seriously as they take themselves. Money we all take seriously, but it could be argued that its misuse harms ourselves rather more than those around us; meanness is self-destructive. Our fellow-Christians we cannot avoid as long as we remain members of a church, and we are always failing to understand how we may reconcile truth with love. We look in this chapter at three areas close to the heart of Christian behaviour where the Christian walks in some peril.

Forgiveness

Acceptance of and forgiveness of the sinner is one of the central themes of the teaching of Jesus. He does not present it, however, as an altruistic demand which human beings must endeavour to practise with one another, but as the consequence of our having been forgiven by God. God is the source of forgiveness and we can choose whether or not to step into our inheritance. Forgiveness is a gift, not an exaction. The parable of the Unforgiving Servant (Matt. 18.23–34), for example, is a precise illustration of this point, though Matthew blurs the story's sharpness by placing it between two apparently exhortatory demands for forgiveness of our brother (vv. 21f., 35).

We always fail our fellow-Christians and all others around us when we will not understand that forgiveness is a gift. We cannot safely forgive one another out of our own resources. When we try, we create dominion. Here are five circumstances in which such a process is seen at work:

(a) 'I will forgive you if you do what I tell you in future'
This is such a naked bid for power that it is strange how frequently people fail to see it as such. It is of course extremely common between parents and children. The parents who play this game make a restoration of relationship dependent upon the child conforming to their demands. Since it is unthinkable for children that they should be deprived of the love of their parents they are forced into compliance. The future cost of that compliance will be a serious, and what appears to the participants to be an inexplicable, rift between parents and child, as the latter violently tries to break free from the love which is so hedged around with conditions yet is still so much needed.

Adults indulge the same habit when any authority is dealing with an erring subordinate. How far it is pernicious here depends first upon whether the participants have been channelled into such relationships by childhood experiences. Where they have, then most usually the authority becomes the stern but forgiving parent and the subordinate the erring but frustrated child. Sometimes a subordinate, who has had the game played against him as a child and now wants the best of both worlds, refuses to take any outward position of authority but blandly intimidates a weak superior from his apparently weak position. We can see those sort of relationships in many a marriage.

The danger of this sort of behaviour becomes less as the rules become more defined. Workmen will obey their foremen not primarily because they tell them to but because both are subject to rules which are independent of either of them. Within the church there is an ambivalence here. There are, or appear to be, rules, but nobody is quite sure what they are; or anyway, there is always some Christian who is prepared to deny that what the church claims to be a rule really is one, or to say that rules are irrelevant for Christians anyway. Grace and law are always a fruitful source of disagreement. So it is difficult for any church superior (bishop, district officer, minister, elder) to say outright, 'I will forgive you if you do what I tell you in future', because the recipients of such a remark can always deny or, if they fear to do that, ignore the authority. In practice then, except in Sunday Schools, this behaviour is not common in church circles, since most church authorities will be saying rather, 'I will forgive you if you try not to do it again.'

It is evident that, where it might be practised, it is a variant of the minister-as-a-parent procedure (see Chapter 4). The difference is that in the context of forgiveness the superior is offered a position of unassailable power over the subordinate since neither party disputes that the latter has sinned. This makes it very dangerous. If, in spite of everything, it is practised ruthlessly by any church authority, it is a sign that it must be as ruthlessly resisted.

(b) *'I will forgive you if you try not to do it again'*

At first sight this appears to be the same as (*a*). It is similar to the extent that it is an attempt to gain supremacy, but it is doing it in a rather more subtle way. In the first example it was simply a matter of 'You will do what I say' while here it is 'I'm a benevolent authority and I'm trying to help you. We both know you have done wrong. Now what you have to try to do is to do better than you have so far managed.' The ground of the appeal has shifted from the authority to the subordinate. There can be no blame attached to the authority because he is concerned for the sinner and he is no longer insisting on blind obedience. Yet he is still trying to build all future relationships in his own image. The purpose of amendment must be in his direction.

An example of this might be a minister in a church large enough to have a junior colleague. The latter one day, incensed beyond prudence, tells an influential member of the congregation just what he thinks of business practices in general and the man's own in particular. The church member summons the minister and complains bitterly at what 'your impertinent young pup' said to him. The minister calls in his colleague, hears his side of the story, says that of course he understands but we cannot really have that sort of un-Christian behaviour in the church. Of course he forgives his colleague but he ought to be careful that that sort of thing does not happen again and please would he go and apologize.

All the participants are deafened by the sound of oil being poured on troubled waters. Everybody is talking about forgiveness but it is being used as a means of suppressing dissent and creating subservience rather than as a genuine process of creating the vulnerability by which they might all discover something more about themselves and the God they serve. The assumptions are that people must never be offended, that business practices are a private affair and not a suitable Christian concern, that youth must give way to age, that forgiveness is always from the superior to the junior. It may be that the young man was unwise, uncharitable and in error but nobody is being allowed the chance to find out.

At least three misunderstandings lie behind this behaviour. The first is a failure to see that the purpose of amendment lies inalienably with the sinner and not with the wronged. Anybody may suggest to, urge upon, a wrongdoer that he should intend to modify his behaviour, but nobody has a right to tell him to do so. He may be told that his behaviour will not be tolerated in such-and-such circumstances and that therefore his continued holding of his office may depend upon his changing, but to enforce choice is logically a contradiction. Secondly, there is a lack of recognition that forgiveness cannot be bought and sold. If we do improve, it is the result of forgiveness and not the price we pay for it. To demand a price renders forgiveness void. Thirdly, the story illustrates that quaint article of faith which says that apologies must always be made upwards. The lesser must make restitution to the greater. The junior colleague must make his apologies to the minister and the influential church member. It scarcely crosses anybody's mind that forgiveness might rightly flow in the contrary direction, too. Whoever heard of a bishop apologizing to his clergy, or a minister to his people, unless it were forcibly dragged out of him? Yet it is obvious that occasions for forgiveness arise among the powerful as much as, if not more than, among the weak. For the powerful to recognize that and to cultivate the habit of admitting their failures does not have the result, as might be expected, of undermining their authority but rather of enhancing their credibility.

(c) 'You'll forgive me, won't you?'

Forgiveness games are also played the other way round, from the sinner to the wronged. It may be a device for wringing concessions out of the wronged like the erring husband who seeks a display of being forgiven by his wife for no other reason than that he wants to make love to her. He relies for getting his own way on his wife's commitment to the marriage. Those who practise this behaviour in a Christian context rely upon the other's commitment to the religious principle of forgiveness.

We may imagine a woman who has been appointed leader of a · ladies' group in a local church. She is good-hearted, inefficient and indolent. She takes so long preparing the year's programme that she misses all the best speakers, she fails to confirm dates with those she finally engages and she arrives at meetings without having prepared any of the details. She beams amiably down upon her members and says that she is so sorry, things seem to have gone wrong again. She doesn't know how it always happens to her but she's afraid the speaker hasn't turned up once more so perhaps the members won't mind having a lovely chat together instead. 'You *will* forgive me, my dears', she ends (this sort of behaviour is frequently accompanied by inappropriate endearments and radiant smiles).

The implication is that the members, being Christian, must forgive everything. All her inadequacies as a leader are to be hidden behind and justified by the demand for forgiveness. Forgiveness is to declare her innocent. The facts that speakers receive garbled instructions, that dozens of women have unexpectedly dreary evenings, that the group is going downhill, that their finances are in a mess, are all to be reckoned as of minor account against the over-riding requirement to forgive. Failure itself comes to have something admirable about it because it becomes the occasion for forgiveness. Luther's 'Sin more strongly that forgiveness may abound' is an element in the forgiveness relationship between human beings as well as between us and God.

The members meanwhile are either seething with frustration or quietly leaving the group. They are disabled from taking the action that is required by the plea for forgiveness. What they should do is either to assist her in her difficulties, to confront her with her shortcomings or to sack her, but we can imagine the reproachful spirit with which she might receive any of those approaches. What Christians are liable to do is to argue in themselves and with one another that 'we must separate the sinner from the sin'. The leader is unquestionably incompetent and runs a meeting appallingly but she is a pleasant person so we will all just do the best we can. It isn't her fault she's so unbusinesslike, they remark.

That sounds very considerate, very Christian, and what truth there is in loving the sinner but not the sin lies in the fact that we are each of us given at birth a character which is amenable to radical change but only within the range of possibilities available to such a character. It may therefore be true that nothing on God's earth would ever make the ladies' group leader efficient. What is dangerous about the argument is that it lets us off the hook. It makes it possible for us to retreat into a mythical world where sin inhabits us like a toad in a summerhouse. We can disclaim responsibility for whatever in ourselves we do not like. The group leader is permitted to evade the task of coming to terms with the incompetence which belongs to her, and of discovering how much of it she might be enabled to overcome.

(d) 'Forgive and forget'

Many Christians are well aware of the 'forgive and forget' trap because it is so common inside and outside the church, so we need not delay long over it here. It is a trite formula employed to short-circuit human interaction.

It is absurd because it is not within the power of humankind to keep a lasting control over memory. We cannot decide to forget. If we forget, we forget and if we do not, we do not. It may be that everything that has happened to us – and some believe that has happened to our long-distant ancestors too – is buried somewhere deep within our unconscious. The circumstances in which these memories are brought to the surface are tangential – a scent brings back the long-forgotten face of a one-time girl friend, a certain word in a book reminds us of a paternal rebuke in our childhood. Remembering and forgetting is a problem not for our conscious self but for our psyche to deal with.

People who say 'Forgive and forget' pretend that they have complete control over their memories and claim all the magnanimity for having initiated reconciliation at the expense of any serious consideration of the differences that have arisen. To pursue the matter after the formula has been repeated looks like an attempt to cast doubt upon the other's integrity, an obtuse determination to revel in wrongdoing, and it will be received with irritation. Yet the likelihood is that the curtailment of the conversation has come exactly at the point when the participants are under some pressure. If they had been prepared to bear the anxiety of persisting there may have been a chance of deeper understanding on each side. The proponent, however, has no wish to make any further commitment and cuts short the relationship, leaving his partner, maybe, with a sense of guilt if he finds himself unable to bring his memory under any sort of control. He cannot forget. Has he therefore not forgiven?

(e) 'Of course I forgive you'

This is punitive forgiveness. It may happen between adults, one of whom is a practising Christian and the other an apparently conspicuous wrongdoer.

A man, for instance, has been going through a painful divorce. Soon after he remarries, when he is still in a somewhat tender state of mind, he is hailed in the street by an acquaintance, a prominent member of the local church. She commiserates with him over his troubles and then, looking serious, remarks, 'Of course, I'm a Christian, as you know, and I thought I would like you to know that I forgive you for what you have done and I will keep on loving you just the same.' There is no insincerity there, rather a certain courage in referring to painful matters so openly, yet it leaves the man in a state of cold fury. Why?

The woman, in a very few words, has successfully established her ascendancy. She has cast the man into the role of sinner and herself into the good Christian whose privilege it is to forgive. The fact that she is, and is seen to be, sincere makes it very difficult for the man to blast back at her that he does not need her forgiveness, thank you, which would restore some of the equality between them. That would be felt by both of them to be ill-natured, even shocking.

So the man is rendered impotent and angry by an approach which is supposed to be one of joyful acceptance. The situation is made even more taut if the man does not in the least share his interlocutor's belief that divorce is wrong. Somehow a well-meaning Christian act has undermined mutality.

The woman has forgotten that the spring from which reconciliation and forgiveness flow is God's forgiveness of us. It is a spring from which we all need to drink and which can only flow through us, not from us. Only when we feel that gift at the root of our beings, when we share personally in the pain of failure and experience God's forgiveness of it, will our forgiveness of others have the ring of truth.

In spite of our natural hesitance, it is probably in the best interests of genuine religion that those who are confronted with this type of behaviour should gather their courage and resolutely defy any reconciliation based upon piety rather than upon God.

Sacrifice

When Christians, particularly professional Christians, talk about sacrifice they very quickly run into deep theological water. What happened when Christ was sacrificed for us? What is the meaning of atonement, propitiation, expiation? What is the nature of the sacrifice of the eucharist? Happily we do not need to flounder in such controversial seas in order to understand the relatively simple conduct we are concerned with here.

Not that it is easy to forget how closely the idea of sacrifice, even for those who are not Christian, is tied up with the figure of a man hanging on a cross, or to underestimate the profound depths by which we may be linked to those who once almost universally (but now rarely) killed animals in ritual form because in no other way could they express what they felt about the meaning of life. Nevertheless, we use the word 'sacrifice' here in its popular sense. We take it to mean the choosing, against the grain but for what seems to us to be a sufficiency of good reasons, of a hard and stony path when other alternatives are available. It is therefore sacrifice in this sense when a wife decides that she will give several years of her life to the bearing and nurture of children when a much-desired and fulfilling career was open to her instead, or when a young person foregoes a university place in order to nurse an ailing parent.

It is worth bearing in mind at this point that the concept of sacrifice is sometimes used in ill-advised ways when people are considering their own claims of conscience. There was, for instance, the young theological student, intelligent and gifted, who looked all set for a bright academic career and did himself feel very attracted to that call. Shortly before he was ordained, however, he felt obscurely that he ought to sacrifice his calling as an academic in order to serve the parochial ministry and offered himself for that purpose. After serving some years it gradually dawned on him that he had made the wrong choice, but by then of course it was too late to return to the university world and he sat out his forty years' ministry in a job to which he never felt really suited. The mistake he made was to imagine that sacrifice must be of something rather than within something. There was plenty of sacrifice to be had in a serious intent to follow an academic calling. The long, lonely hours wrestling with difficult ideas, assessing frankly and without prejudice theories quite different to one's own, the willingness to see one's printed ideas torn to shreds by one's peers, the acute anxiety of aligning one's Christian philosophical ideas with bringing up one's children, with living with one's wife or with worshipping in one's parish church. That is just to mention those common to all academics. Who knows, he may have made the right choice, but a sense of failure carried through life seems an odd way to fulfil a vocation when plain alternatives were available. We need to be clear that there is ample room for sacrifice within any calling without adding unnecessary sacrifices that are marginal or antipathetic to our real life's work. It is far too tempting to adopt marginal sacrifices as a means of evading those closer to home.

However, that is a solitary misuse of sacrificial concepts and I am concerned here with how Christians use sacrifice misleadingly in their dealings with one another. In that context the first example arose in my mind in rather a curious place. I was reading the story in the Acts of the Apostles of the release of St Peter from prison by the angel who, we are told, unfastened his chains, led him out through locked doors and delivered him back to the church. At the end of the story Luke writes:

> When morning came, there was consternation among the soldiers: what could have become of Peter? Herod made close search, but failed to find him, so he interrogated the guards and ordered their execution (Acts 12. 18, 19).

It was the habit in those days to make guards personally responsible with their lives for the safety of prisoners under their care, but it chilled me nevertheless to reflect that Peter's miraculous escape resulted directly in the deaths of several innocent men and that the church is not recorded as having had any qualms of conscience about them. Thoughtlessly the men were sacrificed for Peter (I do not make any judgment about the likelihood of the story as it stands; the central point is that Luke recorded it without any sense of disquiet).

As unthinkingly, people today drag others down the path of sacrifice imagining that the sacrifice is their own. A man is converted at an evangelical rally and at once begins to get caught up seriously in church activities. He goes to Bible studies, house meetings, district conventions and church twice on a Sunday. His wife and family, who are genuinely but conventionally Christian and have not become engaged in his enthusiasms, bear his change with fortitude. In a couple of years the minister invites the man to become a lay pastor in the church. This will involve him in at least another two evenings a week and several training weekends a year. As he talks it over with his wife he says, 'You must see, dear, that this is a sacrifice the Lord is asking of me. I have no choice but to follow his will.' It depends upon what stuff his wife is made of how she answers this plea but the right question to ask is always, 'Who is being sacrificed?'

The man is making a bid to take total control of his own direction of life, whether or not it is at the expense of his other responsibilities, and to do it in the name of an unchallengeable calling. The blossoming lay pastor calls his sacrifice the unambiguous call of God which cannot be resisted, but that sets his family and his other obligations outside God's care. It leaves the

wife with the choice between, in some sense, losing her husband
or following him – in practice a recipe for lifelong tension and
dissimulation. If she wants to make an issue of his lay pastorship
she has to take on God. This is what makes such struggles so
particularly poignant in the church. It is bitter enough if a woman
feels that her husband is sacrificing his family for the sake of his
business, but at least she is able to give battle fair and square,
the family versus the business. If he says it is a call from
God she becomes pinned to the man's creed like a struggling
butterfly.

It must be added that the religious quest is a very serious and a
very lonely one, and it may lead us to detach ourselves in many
ways from that which we find most desirable and lovable. Jesus
made that blindingly clear. When we hear of somebody 'living a
sacrificial life' let those closely involved with him or her judge
whether it is a pilgrimage or a manipulation. They will know.

The next example is another of those, by now becoming familiar,
in which a Christian upstages an opponent in order to keep him
or herself in the right. An old aunt dies and the relations gather
hungrily around her possessions. She has left a will but one couched
in vague terms which does not specify items of furniture, so there
is abundant room for altercation. One of the relations is a middle-
aged man, a regular member of his local church, who attends the
share-out with something of a lofty air as if possessions were of no
account. However, the rest of them notice that he is not slow to
stake his claims. There is some doubt over the disposal of certain
items because not all the relations were able to attend the family
gathering, and in particular over a Jacobean oak chest which, after
some uncertainty and argument, in the end goes to our church
member.

A month later, when the chest is very handsomely adorning his
entrance hall, he gets a phone call from one of the relations who
was not present at the allocation of goods. She says that she does
not want to make a fuss but she understands he has the Jacobean
chest and her aunt did make it very clear to her on several occasions
that she wanted her to have the chest. She has not actually had
anything else from the will so she wonders . . .? After a pause the

man says, 'It's a pity you couldn't have been present at the share-out like everybody else. I mean it's really rather difficult now having got the thing all the way over here. I don't think I received more than my fair share, though of course I didn't know Auntie like you did.' Having made these apparently inconsequential remarks which are in reality oblique but plain objections, he pauses again. Then, 'Of course I'm the last person in the world to stand in the way of anybody's rights and if you really think you are entitled to it then naturally I must give it up.'

His relative is now placed in a most awkward position, as he fully, albeit unconsciously, intended. She has picked up the hints that it is her fault she did not put in an earlier claim, that she is putting everybody to a lot of inconvenience and that it is uncharitable of her to rely upon any special place she may have had in her aunt's affections. She has also heard him allude indirectly to his known Christian commitment. If she persists in her demand she is made to feel stubborn and acquisitive, so she is tempted to say, 'Oh let's forget about the whole thing' and ring off. If she does that he has done well for himself. He has been generous in his willingness to sacrifice the chest, he has put her in the wrong for having asked for it – and he has kept the chest! If she perseveres and he has to relinquish the chest he releases it with a sense of virtue triumphant, and her possession of it becomes in some obscure sense culpable.

This ploy is more irritating than damaging except to the man himself. It is quite difficult to counteract without adding to the sense of injured pride. Probably the best weapon is spontaneous laughter, against which pomposity always has a difficult passage.

A third set of complications clusters round the idea of suffering. The suffering martyr, for instance, is a familiar and tiresome figure. 'Hello!', we say, adding unwisely, 'and how are you?' It is not just that we know on the instant they are going to tell us exactly how they are, we also see how they plan to do it. They fix us with a melancholy smile and say in a soft, thin voice, 'Not very well, I'm afraid. Of course it's nothing really and I'm sure I shall be all right soon but I don't think anyone appreciates quite what it is like . . .'

We smile at the faces that anecdote brings to our minds. Maybe we are less aware how often we play the same game more stealthily. We come home from work, sink into an armchair and when our son asks us to give him a hand with his homework we look momentarily cross, sigh and rise wearily, delivering a silent message every child will instantly recognize. We act in this way whenever events or people or God do not seem to be giving us the satisfactions we need and we seek some sympathy.

The childhood model is the young person who looks for the love and attention of his parents. Like the child we seek recognition from our peers or superiors, and if we do not get it we force them into noticing the burdens we bear. It is a straight manipulative exercise and, like all such, feeds upon itself. We are obliged to act like this because most people find it difficult to ask for the attention they need. Many of us, particularly if we are men, are brought up to believe that we should stand on our own feet, that to seek for affection is at best faint-hearted and probably unhealthy. Our needs remain, however, and because we are forbidden by taboos from making an open bid we have to do it in an underhand way, reaching our requirements by way of our impediments. The counteraction to such behaviour therefore is on the one hand to reach under the manipulation, so to speak, and to try and discover, and meet, the needs that the manipulation conceals, and on the other hand, to let it be known candidly that we have needs too and we would like them satisfied. This latter move will cause any energetic martyr soon to seek a less demanding ear.

Practised between people who have some self-awareness this sort of behaviour is not at all damaging and can in fact be quite appealing. One partner in a marriage, say the wife, has been working intensively for some months having just taken up a full-time job again now the children are at school. She therefore catches influenza as it goes its rounds, and her husband, in face of her protests, packs her off to bed. There she sighs, sinks back upon her pillows and thinks, 'This is good'. Her husband rushes round, leaving meals for her, making her bed and in general treating her as the dependent child she has temporarily become. She luxuriates in her role but both are aware, by means of their shared grins, that this is a game which is delightful but strictly temporary. Each is recognizing that there is a child in all of us who sometimes needs nurturing, but the husband would rightly protest if she did not in due course resume her responsibilities as an adult.

Other sickroom conduct can be destructive where the patient creates a permanent disability from temporary indisposition, pretending all the time that he or she is doing no such thing, or struggles manfully against an illness with a stiff upper lip until collapsing, thus proving how hard he or she was trying and how insensitive the family were not to have noticed it before. In a Christian household it can happen like this: The patient lies in bed, a large crucifix hanging above his head. 'I am identified,' he thinks to himself, 'with our Lord in his suffering.' And so he might be, but he loses no chance of dropping hints about it where he can. He may be either sweetly demanding ('I know it's an awful bother, dear, but do you think I could have a tray?') or sweetly undemanding ('I didn't call you, precious, because I know how busy you are'). He becomes an *alter Christus,* another Christ. To cause any distress to him then is a double offence, against him and against God. Those who tend him smart under the inhibitions this lays upon them and the sickroom becomes a sort of shrine which people enter as if they are going to church.

And so we arrive back at the Christian's attitude to the hurts in life. Without going over ground that we have already covered, it is only necessary here to remind ourselves that plenty of suffering will befall us without our going out of our way to look for it and that Christ, though he accepted his suffering, albeit with aversion, did not seek it. He was no hero.

There is an inversion of such conduct in which we create others into waifs and strays. Richard Sennett writes:

The moral status of the victim has never been greater or more dangerous than it is now . . . the notion which flowered in the Romantic era and continues strong today (is) that no person is morally legitimate unless he or she is suffering. The sources of legitimacy through suffering are ultimately to be found in an injury inflicted by someone else or by 'the environment' . . .

This tendency to live off the oppressed for a sense of one's moral purpose is a devious game . . . It is psychological cannibalism (pp. 149–50).

The whole thrust of modern social care is in sympathy with this quotation. Recent social policy in Great Britain is to shut down many residential homes for young people because they are seen to be paternalistic, and to return the disadvantaged young to the community through foster homes as far as possible. For a long time before that many voluntary societies had been travelling the same road, which was why the Waifs and Strays Society, having first turned itself into the Church of England Children's Society, is today pioneering community-based social care schemes. Politically and internationally the issue has not become so plain. In our context we have noticed in an earlier chapter that charities concerned with overseas aid take a great deal of trouble to ensure that people in the recipient countries are those who become responsible for distributing the aid, in order to avoid any hint of paternalism. It is far from certain, however, that this attitude has filtered very far down among the donors or that Christians have come to terms with a Jesus who, displaying a marked lack of interest in contemporary social problems, was able to say, 'Blessed are the poor.'

The inverse conduct, therefore, is to create waifs and strays round about us whose misfortunes, either out of a sense of blazing injustice or in a spirit of benevolent direction, we employ to give a sense of purpose to our lives, to make us feel good. We also want to avoid any challenges to our own way of life by building their life in the image of ours. If we believe in a high standard of living, then it is best for our peace of mind that everybody else should believe in it too.

Two contrary attitudes make us angry. On the one hand we expect the recipients of our charity to be willing to take it, and we have little sympathy for those who refuse our aid on the grounds that they are not convinced they want to adopt our models. The ambivalence here becomes obvious when we consider how difficult it is for us to accept unsolicited gifts from strangers and how resentful we become when they will not receive them from us. On the other hand, if our beneficiaries make such good use of our gifts as to raise them towards, or even above, the sort of status to which we have become accustomed we feel indignant that they are no longer subservient and anxious what their newly discovered freedom might do to us.

Whereas we might be lured into making these dangers an excuse for ceasing to contribute to any charitable cause whatsoever, a better counteraction might be to have a long talk with a person who is involuntarily employed or to accept the next unsolicited, but scarcely wanted, gift that is offered to us to find out what such an acceptance feels like.

Loving

Parents rearing their children leave each of them with a cluster of paradigms, and the child grows into adulthood exploring how much of it he or she feels belongs to him or her and how much should be discarded if possible.

One of the main ingredients of such training for many children is their parents' insistence that they should be kind. Children should look after one another, help the disadvantaged and be considerate to everybody. Parents oblige their children to follow this advice because they are aware that human beings have an equivocal disposition and they know how easy it is to fall into bad habits. They want to encourage the positive side of their children's nature. Unfortunately the more insistent they are – and in particular the more insistent they are without careful accompanying explanations – the more likely it is that the children will repress the aggressive side of their nature to the extent perhaps of becoming blind to it altogether. As they then mature they become very severe with others' wrongdoings, as severe as their parents were with their own. If they catch themselves out in wrongdoing they will be equally severe with themselves, and the attendant guilt often leads them into the church, where they are offered the free forgiveness which salves, but by no means always heals, the wound.

Reinforcement of the parents' demands that they should be kind comes first from the schools, which disseminate teaching about benevolence in the interests of social order among other things, and more especially from the churches. One unquestionable novelty in the teaching of Jesus was his summing-up of the Law in terms of love. The two great commandments were to love God and to love your neighbour. The New Testament shows that this was a message which the first Christians placed immediately at the centre of their ethics. St Paul on several occasions echoed his master's instruction that love was the fulfilling of the Law, and he very largely escaped the Johannine temptation to narrow the principle of love so that it was to become effective only among the brother-hood, that is between Christians. The church ever since, in word if not in practice, has based its morality upon the concept of love. So in the minds of all of us who claim a Christian allegiance our parents' imperatives about the need for kindness are buttressed by those of school and church.

In this way a polarity may emerge between the command to love and the impossibility of achieving it. Governed by the demands of those who require us to love, we kid ourselves, either temporarily or as a condition, into imagining that, in spite of indications to the contrary, we love everybody. 'Because I am a Christian and I am commanded to do so I love everybody.' We go to live in a world of fantasy where we imagine that the whole of our nature, conscious and unconscious, can be made subject to our will. It might, for instance, happen like this.

A group of Christians meets regularly for prayer and Bible study. One evening, to their surprise, they are joined by Matthew, a young man from their church who has not shown any interest in their group before and whom they suspect of being of rather a different turn of mind to theirs. They are effusive in their welcome, however, and are quite relieved when he makes practically no contribution all evening though he listens carefully enough. He leaves early and the rest of the group before they go home say to one another how nice it was to have him and they must really make him welcome. Matthew continues to attend but finds himself oddly out of place. They seem to have a common mind and nod and smile at one another, and at him, as they talk, yet he does not agree with much of what they say. It is difficult to say so, however, in the face of so much accord. He tries, but is met with more nods and smiles and a resumption of their previous discourse.

One evening his patience is exhausted. He does not feel accepted as part of the group, he says briskly. He is becoming very angry with them and do they want him there or not? They look most discomforted and say that of course they want him there. They are Christians and therefore they accept and love everybody who comes whoever they are. They are sorry Matthew is so angry with them because they have done their best, haven't they? That is not a question Matthew can see any way to answering, and shortly he leaves. When he has gone, the group re-forms and falls to prayer. They pray that their eyes may be opened so that they can see their way to helping Matthew since he is obviously in some spiritual distress at the moment. May the Lord bless and prosper their group, they end.

Such a group always acts from a position of safety. The group is secure in its likemindedness. Each knows roughly what the others are going to say, and though the composition of the group may change from time to time its ethos remains the same. They can readily love one another because they know the group is not going to permit any undermining of their defences. Furthermore, from that position they can love anybody else who is seen to be, or can be made to feel, inadequate or inferior.

That would seem to them to be a perversely harsh and erroneous judgement and naturally there is no conscious desire in them either to create weakness or to make exclusions in the demand for universal love. It is just that the need for security, which takes them into the group and away from the threatening isolation of their destructive feelings, makes it essential that they should be able to maintain control. So there is no danger in loving such people as the elderly and young children, all those who suffer some physical, mental or social disadvantage, other groups and individuals who are not Christian, and even Matthew, provided that, and to the extent that, they can transform him into a person who needs help – which we notice they at once achieved in their prayers when he had gone. Others may be seen to be, and may actually be, stronger than they are, and they avoid the risk that that involves by discovering a point of weakness at which to love them. So love becomes a state of willed harmony wherein disagreements, mildly expressed, are acceptable but dislikes are not.

All of us are prone to such behaviour and in order to maintain the position we have to rid ourselves of all that within us which looks likely to clash with the desired harmony. There are several methods of doing this. We can use the wrongdoing, or the potential for wrongdoing, as a stick with which to beat ourselves. The good guy inside us, with whom we identify, looks with disapproval and disgust at the bad guy who is some sort of loathsome intruder. 'Out!' we say, but alas! he won't go, so we shut our eyes to him or take him on in a running battle. Either way will leave us feeling chronic guilt. Another method of maintaining harmony is to assimilate our bad guy with the devil. Whatever our personal views about the existence of the devil or devils, it is obviously easy to use such a concept as a dump for everything in us that we do not wish to lay claim to. 'It is your old man,' as a pious lady once told me roguishly when I was guilty of some misdemeanour in my youth and it took me years puzzling over the identity of this alien elderly gentleman until I at last came upon the allusion in St Paul!

To use an exterior devil or an interior bad guy are both standard ways of dealing with the negative side of our nature. More common than either, however, is the projection into other people of what we do not choose to acknowledge as belonging to us. Consider what happened to Matthew. He had voluntarily taken his place in a warm fellowship, a loving atmosphere where everyone knew the limits of the demands likely to be made of them. He discovered that the very affection rendered it more difficult for an intruder to express any dissentient feelings. He was aware they were good-hearted and well-intentioned, yet he found himself inhibited from disturbing the peace. Like them he was bound by the imperative that he should love his neighbour but he did not experience the reality of love in the way that they did.

When therefore he did eventually speak he made a strong, impatient speech. The group reacted defensively but still, as they saw it, with love. 'We are sorry you have become so angry,' they said crucially at one point. Matthew is the one who is angry, he has disturbed the peace, he has the difficulties and the doubts. He therefore is the sinner and they have no part in it. And from one point of view that is correct, for Matthew has undoubtedly been the one to state what he feels and thereby to cause the disorder. On the other hand it is also true, first, that the group are the other half of the disturbance, for there would have been none had they not unwittingly provoked it; second, that they have made Matthew fully responsible for causing the upset which has taken place; but most importantly, that they have rid themselves of all those hidden fears of theirs, all those parts of them which are unloving and unlovely, and have dumped them on Matthew. He now carries all the weight of their concealed anxieties while they remain pure and 'loving'. The pay-off is their prayer that they might help him in his difficulties (a neat turning on its head of the original projection) or the 'poor Matthew!'s that they exclaim over their coffee afterwards. Nothing has broken into their goodness for they have left everything else with him.

It should perhaps be added that we cannot assume that Matthew is always acting from the purest of motives in attending the group at all. But we should not allow ourselves to perform yet another projection by using Matthew's behaviour as an excuse for failing to recognize our own.

This kind of loving can be counteracted by refusing the open projections of those who practise it (we cannot do much about the hidden ones). The answer to 'Because I am a Christian I love everybody' is 'I'm a Christian and I can't stand Y'. If the rejoinder to that is, 'You ought to love Y', it leads with luck into a discussion about the nature and source of our feelings and of our control over them, while if it is, 'If you can't stand Y you can't be a Christian' it provokes enquiry about the characteristics of Christian commitment.

6 | Non-believers and the Believer

The bulk of this book is a plea that Christians should make an unremitting effort in self-analysis. Committed as we are to a pursuit of the good, we need to be resolute in winkling out all the pretensions, prejudices and pomposities that such a quest often gives rise to. I use the word self-analysis in preference to self-examination because the latter is a loaded word in a Christian context. For Christians, self-examination normally describes the practice of making a list of our endless sins, and that is not a habit, in my opinion, that should have more than a small part in Christian discipleship. Self-analysis strives to make clear to ourselves the sort of person we have become in relation to God, to ourselves and to all those who have formed us, and therefore to give us a better chance of shaping the future. It is a wider exercise than self-examination. It is also a laborious one and, initially at any rate, seems to beget more harm than good. We feel depressed, helpless, and above all confused. It is only slowly, as we cautiously put new insights into practice and discover the growth within the hurts, that refreshing fruits begin to emerge.

The present chapter is a relief from the rigour of that undertaking. Christians are not the only group that will benefit from self-analysis or that is ensnared, through its absence, in self-deceit. I want to look at the Christian faith from the outside looking in, from the position of those who profess little or no religion. I shall be describing two ways in which consciously irreligious people make use of Christians, or indeed anybody else who is following a religious or moral ideal, either to displace or to justify their faithlessness.

Creating an embarrassment

It is no novelty for people to scoff at religion as this quotation from the Book of Psalms (42.9,10) makes clear:

> I will say to God my rock, 'Why hast thou forgotten me?' Why must I go like a mourner because my foes oppress me? My enemies taunt me, jeering at my misfortunes; 'Where is your God?' they ask me all day long.

Anyone who professes faith in God in a scientific age must be prepared for ridicule even more than those ancient and purportedly romantic Jews, who, frozen in their venerable mythologies, did not know any better. Christians are often seen to be no doubt kind-hearted and well-meaning, but stubbornly credulous and faintly ludicrous as well.

Those who mock today will not usually do so with any venom. Unless they have been exposed to an experience of religion in their youth or later which has left them feeling hostile, they will typically approach us in a spirit of bewildered exasperation. When the subject of religion arises in staff canteen, office, staffroom, pub or at a large family gathering they will glance at us to see what the known Christian is going to do. They watch to see if we are to make a contribution. If we do not they may play a sort of off-shore game, seeing how much splashing they can make before we take the plunge, though they will quickly tire of this and change the subject if we refuse to play and stick to the beach. We delay our interjection as long as possible because we know they are waiting for us to make that very first remark, whatever it might be, so that they can begin their mild baiting. As soon as we respond in religious terms they jump in, telling us perhaps that they can only believe in what they can see and feel or relating some story highly embarrassing to the church, past or present.

The game is to see how ticklish a situation they can contrive for us without any personal commitment of their own. They want to see the flush rising from our neck and to hear the shrill tone of our defensiveness. The sly smile at the corner of the mouth will show when their end has been achieved and they will stop at once, the

subject being changed as quickly as possible before any possibility
arises of a real engagement with it.

At this point we should pause to take note of one or two themes
which a little reflection makes plain but which tend to vanish from
our minds when we are under pressure. For instance, we should
not necessarily take an attack of this nature at its face value. Many
people make a genuine religious enquiry under the guise of faint
ridicule because it keeps them safely on known territory. Indiffer-
ence, as we all know, is the opposite of both hate and love, so a
willingness to engage in argument shows a modest care for the
subject at issue. Even if the engagement is in the form of a virulent
attack, displaying some deep-seated hostility, at least its opposite,
positive side becomes potentially accessible. So, while the course
of the encounter requires that the negative ingredient of our
opponent's nature should interlock with our own, we should not
forget that there is another side to both of us. A real search can be
hiding behind a mocking posture. That posture itself is of great
value to those who adopt it because it prevents them having to
examine the issues with any seriousness.

Another point to keep in mind concerns our own attitude to our
faith. If we are totally convinced of the inerrancy of every article
of the Christian faith few will bother to mock us. It is no fun to
engage with a figure of adamantine resolution. If there is any contact at all it will be a straight trial of strength with each side manning
the fortifications. This is why ministers are not often faced with
this sort of attack; they are assumed, not always rightly, to be
rigidly orthodox in their beliefs and quite unsympathetic to any
doctrinal deviation. Most of us, though, have hesitations about
certain items of received truth and think it reasonable to do so. If
we decline to accept teaching on the simple basis that somebody
in authority tells us it is true we have only the alternative of putting
what we are told to the test. That involves periods in which the
doctrine is under our scrutiny, demanding an open mind if our
search is to be a genuine one. It is in this sort of period, or at these
vulnerable points, that the scoffer will lay his traps, often with an
intuitive, devilish accuracy. That is the time for us to listen carefully to what the objector is actually saying, because our fears and

doubts are much more likely to lead us to retreat into a self-justification which has already conceded the objector's point.

Here are three possible reactions to such an encounter which do not involve either a withdrawal into impotent, blushing silence or an advance into an inappropriately strident affirmation of belief. Readers will understand that these are only suggestions for undermining our cross-examiner and in no way prejudge how individuals might wish to speak in detail.

The first approach is to follow every general's rule of thumb and to swing into the attack. The objector's purpose, as I have said, is to make the Christian embarrassed and defensive, so an immediate offensive will wrong-foot him or her. Perhaps offensive is too strong a word. We do not need to be belligerent, only to maintain confidently the beliefs which we hold because we have experienced their truth. Immediately we speak of what we know rather than of what we think we ought to believe it becomes plain that we are on safe ground. Our listeners will infallibly detect the authentic note in what we say and those others present who are sympathetic to our cause may then feel able to join forces with us.

Arising out of that, therefore, we need to be clear about different kinds of knowledge. This is a somewhat complicated field and for our purposes we do not need to do more than distinguish the knowledge verifiable from experience from the knowledge verifiable by experiment. If we want to know the chemical composition of a tree or the technical properties of heat there are certain ways of going about it and assured results at the end of it. We take it for granted that knowledge gained by such experimental methods is acceptable to all rational beings. It may not be very helpful to the lay person but nobody doubts its veracity. The facts of experience, however, are not verifiable by experiment because they have their source in countless individuals. Investigators are trying all the time to discover patterns which are common to all human beings, but their conclusions cannot be measured like tangible things, are always hotly disputed and are constantly negated by individuals who say firmly, 'That is not true for me.'

Our adversary will ridicule if possible the argument that faith is a fact of experience because it demolishes the basis of the position taken, though he or she will be vulnerable if the argument is shifted from faith to love. Only the most cynical, or the strict biological determinists, will deny the splendour and the mystery of the love between man and woman, between friends, between parents and children. They will have experience of it themselves that they cannot deny and it is manifest that it is not open to any kind of proof. Verification to a degree may come from observers who gauge the participants' behaviour to each other but their conclusions have always to give way to what the participants say about it themselves. And that, of course, is exactly the position where belief in God is concerned. So to say how we feel about those we love or to ask the other how he or she feels should considerably advance our case.

Lastly, we are safer with God than we are with the church. The church has been, and is often now, so grotesque and tragic that we cannot fail to be put on the defensive when we talk about it. It is perfectly possible to produce polished arguments about the crusades, the centuries of persecution of the Jews by Christians, the ecumenical impasse and the 'holy war' in Northern Ireland, but we have to be fairly well-informed on historical and contemporary affairs and we are hard pressed to avoid special pleading. We can say what we encounter in the church we live with, the extent to which the support and love of our fellow Christians is satisfying. We can add that we do not expect the church to be perfect, for open admission of faults, in past or present, is disarming. To wander too far away from those narrow paths leaves us hopelessly exposed. We do not expect, and do not wish, to believe in the church in the same way as we have faith in God, and we would be advised not to allow the opposition to manoeuvre us into confusing the two.

The projection of faith and ideals

The second sort of encounter is more dangerous than the last, more subtly undermining. Its essence is that the non-religious person uses the religious both as the guardian of the moral and religious principles he is not prepared to strive for and as the pretext for himself making no effort to labour for them. Perhaps initially we can examine such behaviour more easily in a marital rather than a religious setting.

The principle constituent of all such transactions is the splitting of the good from the bad. A girl is brought up in a family where her parents are strict and her sister is the favoured one. She is not in any way illtreated, yet matures amidst a clear implication that she is in the wrong most of the time. She resists it, yet believes it, and in due course marries a man built in the image of her severe parents. She and her new husband are very fond of one another, but she cannot get out of the way of thinking that he and his principles ought to be paramount while she continues to feel the guilt of always being at fault. He frowns when he comes home from work and finds a pile of nappies in the hall, and she hurriedly pushes them into the kitchen, resentful that he has made her feel bad again and meeting resentment in him because she is not the cheerful, light-hearted wife he needs. Although they tell each other that they know there are faults on both sides, their inner convictions do not allow them to act as if it were true.

The situation becomes more complex if the husband, while maintaining a sense of his own righteousness, is not prepared in practice to pay any more than lip-service to the venture of marriage, yet demands of his wife and family the highest standards and behaviour, enforcing impeccable table manners, an austere domestic routine, regular church-going and abundant good works. (A wife, of course, can do the same thing.) Common sense tells us that he has put himself entirely in the wrong, but in reality he has gained a position of some ascendancy. He can congratulate himself for embracing the highest ideals, reproach his family for not upholding them, use these reproaches as the instance of his adherence to the ideals and so exonerate himself from having to do anything about them himself.

That is one way how it works in marriage, and the same sort of rules apply between the religious and their critics. Many people have, in the widest sense, a spiritual yearning in their hearts which they have no intention of satisfying, for to move out of their accustomed groove is a greater effort than they are prepared to undertake. They need, however, to see themselves as not inferior to their religious neighbours, and the chief way to do that without setting out on a similar trail is to find reasons for demonstrating that those who claim religion for themselves are poor advertisements for their cause. In many cases this is self-evidently true in a personal sense, though it makes no allowances for how different the individual might be without religion. For the non-religious, however, the disparagement is a sign that they are no less upholders of the ideals than the religious and that, since the religious have failed, there is no reason in the world why they should attempt it. They leave, therefore, with the religious all the burden of sustaining the ideal and all the obloquy for having failed to reach it.

The elementary form of this process is the familiar one of 'Why doesn't the church ...?' or 'Why don't the bishops ...?' Any national cause elicits a demand from one section of the public or another that the representatives of the church should do or say something. It is most satisfying, because the church often believes (often rightly) that it has some responsibility in the matter in question, feels guilty because of its previous record in this field, and internally is divided over what the best response might be. A firm statement of principle or a thoughtful but qualified opinion are equally open to ridicule, the one because the church is being rigid and the other because it is weak and vacillating, and they grin at the church's discomfiture.

The church is more heavily protected than the individual Christian, and it is the latter who is more seriously affected, often without being fully aware of it. Church members during the week have to rub shoulders with those for whom they stand as the representative Christian, and the non-religious will be watching for signs both of their piety and of their failures. It is not long before piety becomes a sign that they believe themselves to be superior to their colleagues and failures an indication that they are frauds who do not practise what they preach. The charge of hypocrisy also awaits them if, in order to avoid that dilemma, they choose to play down their piety or to make light of their failures. In the one case they are seen as disloyal and in the other as contemptible. There is virtually nothing they can do or be which is not neatly turned on its head and used in evidence against them.

Where there is natural reticence, which makes it less likely that the non-religious will simply scoff or that it will be counteracted if they do, this sort of encounter can take place without a word being spoken, and the tensions caused by being required to uphold the ideal at the same time as being silently condemned for falling short of it become an internal battlefield. Because people always know they are nowhere as good as they feel they ought to be, the self-reproach which arises out of the recognition of the justice of the unspoken accusation wars with a sense of indignation that it is only they who are being required to follow the ideal, while the other escapes scot-free. For those bold enough to resolve that conflict by expressing anger against the other, the action will at once be taken as confirmation of the argument since anger is seen to be *ipso facto* 'un-Christian'.

People often act like this not, primarily, because they have any particular quarrel with us as individual Christians or even with religion as a whole. Rather they are using us as the means of resolving their own sense of failure in the pursuit of good. It appears as if they are presenting us with our problem whereas in reality they are trying to find a solution to their own. We, however, brought up in churches in which guilt and fear are so often presented as stronger motivations than love and care, unwillingly accept the burden of the ineffectiveness of their pursuit as well as of our own and then wonder why we find the practice of religion such a depressing business.

The technical name for this sort of behaviour is projection, in which subjective qualities which a person does not wish to acknowledge as his or her own are assigned to the objective world. Recognition of such projection is one of the chief ways of handling the behaviour here described. It enables us to distinguish more clearly the enquiries that properly belong to us from those which we have had imposed on us. It is a demanding exercise, yet one which in due course yields liberating fruits. Meanwhile we may question here the assumption that it is ideals and standards that we should rightly be concerned with.

By their nature standards are inflexible and ideals unrealizable. Standards are the principles either by which we have decided to live or which have been imposed upon us; ideals are the beckoning finger of perfection. 'Thou shalt not commit adultery' is a standard, a perfectly harmonious church fellowship is an ideal. Those without religion expect us to have strong principles and high ideals and judge us by how far we fall short of them.

It is by no means clear, however, that this is the Christian call presented in the Bible. Jesus showed a conspicuous lack of interest in right and wrong, preferring to live in the shifting world of good and evil. This world is 'shifting' not because God does not know what is good and what is evil but because humanity cannot clearly perceive it. Jesus knew what it was that defiled a person and where it came from (Mark 7.14ff), and as a direct consequence of that knowledge turned on its head the contemporary conventional view of morality by associating freely with the ritually and morally defiled. There is no guarantee that what we take to be fixed moral principles do not, in the divine wisdom, become something else. We have only to recall that 400 years ago Christians were devotedly burning one another for failing to agree about Christian doctrine or 150 years ago justifying the sending of young children down coal mines all day. Nowadays such behaviour would be as abhorrent as failing to ensure that a severely handicapped person had the means of support, and similar blindnesses without doubt afflict this generation too.

The Christian in the New Testament is not presented as moving throughout life from one fixed end – principles, to another – ideals. Life rather is a pilgrimage starting again and again at the point of faith, moved by the firm hope which is based upon the work of Christ and guided only by the call to love. There are certain things which have generally been found to be true and thereby become principles so that there would be few, for instance, who would encourage us to stub out our cigarettes on the back of a child's neck. There are also yearnings in us which the most stringent search only intensifies and these reveal the call to perfection which Jesus himself ratified (Matthew 5.48). But the Christian life is described as 'The Way', and Jesus' unique demand is not that his disciples should obey him but that they should follow him.

Those who use the Christian in this way attempt to manoeuvre us into a black-and-white world where moral and doctrinal distinctions are sharp and uncompromising. In this way they make the assumption that a defined existence is the call of the Christian, give expression to their own longings for such an existence, avoid any commitment to it and leave the Christian all the responsibility for maintaining it. The counteraction here, therefore, is to refuse to accept the premise. To be a Christian is not to become bound to a set of simplistic orthodoxies which we fail to uphold at the cost of endless guilt, censure and repentance, but rather to become free in the service of a master who at times leads us in an exceedingly odd dance.

7 | Jesus, Emotion and Responsibilty

Every Christian commentator has an understandable wish to claim Jesus on his or her side of the argument. There can be little hope for any approach to the Christian faith which cannot show Jesus to be for us rather than against us. It is therefore my intention in this last chapter to attempt to show that to talk of Christian discipleship in the terms I have used in this book is at the very least compatible with what we know of Jesus through the Gospels. I would myself go further than that. I have come to believe that much of the behaviour I have described can be a destructive exercise and is one of the foremost ways in which Christians deny themselves the gift of that 'abundant life' that Jesus promised us, and that the slow and painful process of discovering the manoeuvres we engage in produces rich fruit. But I do not believe that the pursuit of these aims should become an exclusive or even a principle aim of our lives. Jesus is, I believe, free of any attempt to manipulate people in such a way but he arrives there not by an earnest attempt to avoid such behaviour but by a precise identification and pursuit of the true goals. That is, in principle, a good example to follow.

Since, however, our pursuit of the true goals will not be as singleminded as Jesus's, it will be helpful if we have some idea of the reasons why Jesus does not fall into the traps and we do. Why do we play so many destructive games and how does Jesus avoid them? Part of the answer to that seems to me to lie in two facts. We are afraid of our emotions and we are afraid of becoming responsible. Jesus is afraid of neither.

If we run our minds over some of the procedures that have been described, we can see how many of them we practise in order to avoid direct emotional contact with people. We cannot risk admitting what we really feel because it makes us too vulnerable. We cultivate evasive prayer, for instance, because to fall to prayer is easier than to encounter real people making demands of us, or we retreat into a safe, religious world because it is so much less exacting than the real one (see Chapter 2). We use forgiveness in a number of different fashions as a device for closing off avenues we do not wish to explore. 'Forgive and forget' shortcircuits human relationships at the very point where they are likely to become fruitful but disturbing. 'You'll forgive me, won't you?' claims an acceptance which must remain, if not blind, at least dumb to any faults (see Chapter 5). When a minister establishes ascendancy, relationships are created in accordance with a formula in which all parties feel safe. The hurts of hierarchical confrontation are preferred to those of personal exposure (see Chapter 4).

Jesus seems to have been perfectly comfortable with his emotions. He stood at the entrance to the tomb where his friend, Lazarus, lay dead, surrounded by ritually mourning Jews and accompanied by Lazarus's two sisters, Mary and Martha, weeping bitterly for their brother, and he wept with them all. More than that, St John reflects accurately at this point the way that the other three gospels, especially St Mark, speak of the inner life of Jesus. St John does not speak only of Jesus weeping (compare Luke 19. 41) but uses words (John 11.33) which seem to talk of a strange sort of indignation alongside an inner turmoil of spirit. What St John thought Jesus was angry about here or what he imagined caused the inward anguish is peculiar to his own special view of the work of Jesus. Perhaps it concerned the onlookers' faithlessness about that which Jesus was able to do and immediately, in St John's account, showed himself capable of doing. Whatever the interpretation, there is no doubt that John rightly speaks of Jesus's capacity to show strong emotion, just as the other gospels do.

St Mark, commonly taken to be the first of the gospellers, refers constantly to Jesus's inner feelings. When Jesus healed the leper (Mark 1.41) the more strongly supported reading says that Jesus's 'heart went out to him', and the word used comes from precisely

the same root as that which Jesus himself preferred when, in the
story of the Prodigal Son (Luke 15.11–32), he told of the father
who saw his errant son in the far distance and was 'strongly moved'
and ran to meet him. The root of the word strictly means 'intes-
tines' and we today use the word 'guts' in the same way as the seat
of the stronger emotions. A little later on, in a similar sort of situation, when Jesus was about to heal a man with a withered hand St
Mark records (Mark 3.5), that he was furious with the Jews who
were more concerned about upholding the law of the sabbath than
they were with the cure of the sick man. Jesus 'looked round at
them angrily, very upset that their hearts were so calloused'. It
was a constant complaint of Jesus that the Pharisees were 'hard-
hearted', that is, that they did not allow emotion to intrude upon
principle.

St Mark's version of the rebuke of St Peter (Mark 8.32, 33) is
another interesting example. St Matthew (Matthew 16.23, 24)
emasculates a story that is more powerful in St Mark. Peter is
horrified to hear Jesus speaking about his suffering and death. He
needs to make a protest but does not wish to upbraid him publicly
so he 'took Jesus to one side'. Jesus was having none of it. He
'turned himself round', refusing the privacy of the quiet word, and
'looking at his disciples', rebuked Peter in turn, making it known
openly how vulnerable he was to the devilish temptation to choose
the easy road.

His affectionate love for people scarcely needs chronicling. It
was one of the main reasons why ordinary people took to him so
well and why the contemporary authorities found him so disturbing and eventually crucified him. He hugged the children in the
teeth of his disciples' opposition (Mark 10.16, Matthew did not
much care for that and simply said that Jesus placed his hand on
them, Matthew 19.15). He touched people all the time – the ritually
(and no doubt factually) unclean, like the leper (Mark 1.41), the
tongue of the deaf-mute (Mark 7.33), even the bier of a dead man
(Luke 7.14), and the frightened, like the three disciples hearing
the disembodied voice on the mount of the transfiguration (Matthew 17.7). He allowed himself to be touched, for the crowd
recognized that there was power in the touching of him (Luke 6.19,

etc. – compare the woman with the internal haemorrhage Luke 8.44–48). He had no fear of discriminating in love. At certain moments he would be overwhelmed with love for particular people like the rich young man (Mark 10.21) or the widow at Nain (Luke 7.13, the 'guts' word here again), and St John has no doubt that Jesus had a favourite disciple (John 21.20).

Nor did Jesus have any trouble with other people's emotions. One of the most noticeable things about his behaviour was the way he insisted on meeting challenges openly even when they were put obliquely. So many of those who surrounded Jesus, whether friends, enemies or suppliants, behaved just as we do when something lies between us and another person. They shrank from an open confrontation, but made their views known through a third party, or they complained among themselves without involving the principal, or they made their disapprobation known through pursed lips. Thus the official at the synagogue was angry with Jesus because he had healed on the sabbath day (Luke 13.14) but he redirected his anger towards the people and berated them for their disobedience because he was afraid of tackling Jesus directly. Or again when James and John asked for a special place in Jesus's kingdom (Mark 10.35–45) or when, shortly before his death according to St Matthew's account (Matthew 26.6–13), a woman poured a jar of expensive perfume over Jesus's head, the disciples became very angry and muttered about it to one another. On each of these three occasions Jesus took the initiative in bringing the cause for contention out into the open. On another occasion when the disciples were talking about precedence (Mark 9.33–37) Jesus had to plough his way through their obstinate determination to say nothing at all. A final example of the covertly censorious approach is the Pharisee who asked Jesus to dinner but would not openly express his disapproval of the fact that Jesus had not performed the ritual lustrations before he sat down to eat, though Jesus immediately took him up on it (Luke 11.37ff.).

Jesus could receive love as easily as he gave it. St Luke tells us (Luke 7.36–50) of the dinner party at the house of Simon the Pharisee, visited by the notorious sinner who wept at Jesus's feet and poured oil on his feet. He showed no sign of embarrassment at such unexpected effusiveness. He used the occasion to give penetrating teaching to his host and loving acceptance to the woman.

Jesus was at home with his emotions, the negative ones as well as the positive. He had needs and he had demands and he did not, through fear of the consequences, conceal either. He did not ask for one thing in terms of another nor did he make any pretence about what he wanted. He indulged in no emotional blackmail. He often needed to be by himself to pray, so he made time for it at the expense of those who might need him and without making any excuses to his disciples (Mark 1.35–38). He often made people feel angry, sad, confused, frightened, amazed and accepted. At times he also made them feel ashamed because their grasp of what he was trying to show them was so slight (for example, Matthew 15.16, 17). But I do not believe it can be shown that he ever made anyone feel guilty. The shame that Jesus sometimes brought about was never a diffused inhibiting guilt but was always directed to a particular end, the strengthening of a stated purpose.

Those who are on the way to becoming comfortable with their emotions are normally people who are also learning about becoming responsible for themselves. A responsible person in this sense is one who is prepared to stand alone, unprotected, where he or she happens to be and to act for themselves from that position. Such a person is not prepared to shoulder the responsibility that properly belongs to somebody else nor is afraid to accept what belongs to him or her. If we look back again briefly at some of the behaviour described in this book we shall see how the fear of becoming responsible or the attempt to shift responsibility onto others or the denial of responsibility to others lies at the heart of many of them.

We looked at the situation where people choose churches like restaurants (see Chapter 2). We wish to worship, and look round to find the easiest available option because we do not want to be confronted with practices, ideas or people which might threaten the norms to which we have become accustomed. We want to hide behind what we would like to be rather than to take the responsibility of discovering who we are. The two friends who had to accept as a gift what they had requested as a charge on them were, in the nicest possible way, denied the right of managing their own affairs (see Chapter 3). Others make a bid, sometimes deliberately, to take responsibility from others under the guise of consulting them and then self-righteously complain when their mock exercise produces nothing but fury in the recipients (see Chapter 4). The evangelically converted man accepts whole-heartedly the religious choice which God lays before us but at the expense of his responsibility to others who have a rightful claim on him (see Chapter 5).

One of the most responsible things we can do, perhaps the only responsible step we can take, is to choose. As soon as we choose, are seen to have chosen and are prepared to accept the consequences of having done so we become responsible human beings. Every way he knew Jesus reinforced the message that men and women must choose. Primarily he made that message clear by living it. Nobody who reads the Gospels can fail to feel the breathtaking urgency that surges through Jesus's short ministry. The kingdom was to be preached, men and women were to be healed, the current interpretation of the Law had to be challenged, disciples must be chosen and prepared, ordinary people had to be offered the opportunity of new life. Relentlessly Jesus pursued these aims. Insistently and sometimes with impatience but never in a hurry, he sought the Father's will, wherever that might lead, quickly coming to feel that time was running out. Three times, so our Gospels tell us, he warned his disciples that he would soon be taken from them and killed, and they could scarcely hear him.

If he was himself a living example of the paramountcy of choice he was also not afraid to exercise that choice in particular circumstances. We have become so used to the story of the call of the twelve apostles that we rarely pause to reflect what a singular sort of exercise it was. Evangelists today do not normally select twelve strangers to act as their back-up team. They expect evidence of conversion and of stability in the faith and upon that basis they may be prepared to make an appointment. Ministers will often do even less than that. They will ask for volunteers and keep their fingers crossed that the Lord will send them somebody sensible. Jesus needed twelve disciples and chose certain men to act in that capacity. It was deliberate and it was risky. He may be supposed to have had a good deal more insight than the rest of us (often it is said how he 'knew their thoughts') but that did not relieve him of the chance of making mistakes. We know that he made at least one bad choice and the behaviour of all the others we are told about came pretty near to scuppering his entire ministry. That is the chance he took and he was prepared to carry the consequences on his own shoulders. Nor was it a one-sided choice. The call to the disciples was not an act of mesmerism. It was a free call to free men who could themselves choose how they responded to it. No doubt they thought themselves greatly privileged but we would not expect to be told of any whom Jesus called and they refused, would we?

So Jesus was himself comfortable in the realm of choice and he urged it upon his hearers. The story of the Good Samaritan (Luke 10.25–37) is a familiar example of the way he turns the tables upon his questioners so that they are forced to make a choice. Asked, 'Who is my neighbour?', Jesus ended up his story with the question, 'Who was neighbour?' That is, he insisted that the real problem facing his questioner was not the nature of racial or religious differences but whether the man was prepared to act upon what he already knew. Often Jesus ends a parable with a question, throwing the response back at the listeners. 'Are you jealous because I am kind?' he ends the story of the workers in the vineyard (Matthew 20.15), or 'What is the meaning of this scripture?' he asks the people who cannot believe the harshness of the judgment meted out to the tenants of the vineyard (Luke 20.17), or again when he mocks the rich fool who has built himself vast storehouses but cannot fill them because he is going to die, 'Who will benefit from all your preparations?' (Luke 12.20).

Similarly Jesus confronted his hostile questioners with the fact of choice. An illuminating example is the challenge made about the source of his authority (Mark 11.27–33). Where did he get the authority to speak as if he knew it all and to act with such disregard for the conventions of the Jewish faith? The question was a very serious one and Jesus did not answer it irritably, as he sometimes appeared to do with questioners (Matthew 22.29), but with careful attention. Yet, again his answer came in the form of a question.

The Jewish religious authorities were trying to nail him with a charge of blasphemy if he were to claim divine authority for what he taught and did. Yet they themselves had at least tacitly accepted the teaching and the baptism which John the Baptist practised (Mark. 1.5) and they themselves may even have been baptized by him (Matthew 3.7). They accepted therefore that there were some people, particularly one like John the Baptist who had the advantage of looking and behaving like the traditional Old Testament prophet, who were outside conventional religion but who had a genuine message. If they had accepted John, was the implication of Jesus's question, why not himself? In this way Jesus's questioners were turned back once again to their own search. 'What do you choose to believe? Who do you choose to follow?'

A superficial observer might imagine that Jesus was almost embarrassingly casual over whether his message got through or not. There was no mistaking the urgency on his side but he frequently made the remark, 'Let him hear who has ears to hear', as if it did not matter to him whether they heard or not. It is on the contrary a marvellous example of Jesus's clear understanding of the nature of responsibility. Many a present-day protagonist of the faith confuses the urgency of the message with the response it elicits in the hearers. The one becomes dependent on the other. If preaching produces the response expected the hearer at once becomes hobbled to whatever doctrine the preacher is propounding and the preacher is reinforced in his or her convictions, while the continued absence of the reaction sought will lead the preacher to agonize despairingly or to withdraw self-righteously. Jesus made no such mistake. He kept a clear distance between the preaching and the response. The earnestness, almost at times the implacability, of his message is not in doubt. That was the task clearly and devastatingly laid upon Jesus. The response to that message lay totally within the responsibility of his hearers. Jesus had no part in the response to his message. As he said to the people when they were looking to the clouds for interpretations of existence, 'Why don't you judge for yourselves the right thing to do?' (Luke 12.57).

A final example of Jesus's understanding of how responsibility works comes in the story of the rich young man (Mark 10.17–27).

He came running up to Jesus one day and fell dramatically to his knees before him. 'Good teacher!' he exclaimed, 'what shall I do to claim my heavenly-life inheritance?' Jesus did not immediately answer the question. First he shot back, 'Why do you call me good?' The young man had one excellent reason for calling Jesus good. He wanted a 'good teacher' because then he could opt out of all personal responsibility. If the teacher is good then he is *ipso facto* authentic and any options about following him fall by the wayside. Needs must. You are the master now and I am the subject. I will either follow you and obey you completely or I will withdraw from you and complain that you were not right after all. If you are a good teacher it is not my responsibility any longer, it is yours.

That was the game the young man was playing. He did not wish to make a choice, he wished to be compelled to choose, thereby negating his ostensible quest. Jesus saw through it at once. 'There is nobody good, except one, and that's God.' Goodness inheres in God alone. If the young man wanted to follow God then that must be his own personal response and not even Jesus could act as an intermediary in his choice. It was for this reason that Jesus continued surprisingly by referring the man back to the Mosaic law as if final salvation was to be found there. 'You know the commandments: "Do not commit murder . . ."' If he required an external authority to do his faith for him then, as a Jew, he had one already and there was no point in adding the burden of a further teacher to his conscience. 'But teacher, I've *done* all that since I was a boy,' the young man cried out, with the agonized implication that it had not been a satisfying quest. That drew the love from Jesus when he saw that he might be prepared to forsake law for grace. 'You are lacking one thing. Go . . . sell . . . come . . . follow.' And he could not.

good luke
serk.